"Vic Sarin is one of the finest cinematographers Canada has ever produced."

— The Right Honourable Adrienne Clarkson

"Judging by the way Vic Sarin's richly composed images haunt the mind, at least a part of the national film industry has already arrived."

— John Bemrose, *Macleans Magazine*

"Sarin is a master cinematographer and *Desert Riders* is a beautiful film."

— John Mackie, *Vancouver Sun*

"A project that took Sarin more than a decade to get made, *Partition* looks and feels like it comes from the heart and as old-fashioned as it might sound, that still goes a long way."

— Janet Smith, *Georgia Straight*

"In *Heartaches*, Vic Sarin's cinematography is superb. The pearly, overcast shots are worthy of Ansel Adams."

— Jay Scott, *The Globe and Mail*

"*Chautauqua Girl*, the best television program of the year... Vic Sarin made it an enchanting experience on screen."

— Ross McLean, *Montreal Gazette*

"Vic Sarin has trained his cameras on dazzling Prairie sunsets and the sweeping landscape to produce a sun-bathed enticement to cancel Club Med plans and book two weeks in southern Alberta.... Some of Sarin's exterior shots are as stunning as oil paintings."

— Mike Boone, *Montreal Gazette*

"*Coming and Going* is a sensitive treatment of a serious problem, one that we will all face; dying. To get inside this situation is an accomplishment for Cherniak and Sarin. The images of hands holding hands and the faces — pensive, crying laughing — will live with me for a long time."

— Charles Lazer, *Cinema Canada*

"*Margaret's Museum*, the third feature by Nation Film Board-trained director Mort Ransen, flaunts the Cape Breton region's pristine and dramatic landscape like never before through Vic Sarin's lush cinematography."

— John Hopkins, *Halifax Mail Star*

"In *Margaret's Museum*, the seductive beauty of the picturesque Cape Breton community is highlighted at every turn by Vic Sarin's gloriously affectionate cinematography."

— Michael D. Reid, *Victoria Times Colonist*

"In *Dancing in the Dark,* Vic Sarin's camera work is always the detached observer and without calling attention to itself, subtly changes mood from house to drab hospital, from bright colours to dark ... no gesture is wasted, neither is one camera shot. All technical credits are first-rate."

— Cannes Film Festival Reviews.

"*Cold Comfort* is a red-hot coup. Vic Sarin, making his feature debut as a director in *Cold Comfort*, does a marvelous job of freeing the material from its theatrical origins without once damaging the roots. Sarin uses his camera to explore the Western landscape – and Sarin the cinematographer is the Canadian master of that scene. The play, the adaptation, the performances, the direction, this is a film where everything falls immaculately into place."

— Rick Groen, *The Globe and Mail*

"Where the film *(Bye Bye Blues)* really shines is in Vic Sarin's cinematography with its artfully composed framing, discreet camera movements, and effective use of the distinctive Alberta light ... visually it's gorgeous."

— Fred Haeseker, *The Calgary Herald*

"One of the two best things (*The Long Road Home*) ... Vic Sarin's stunning and painterly cinematography."

— Ray Conlogue, *The Globe and Mail*

"*Artemisia* was written, directed and produced by Adrienne Clarkson ... lovingly filmed with a painter's eye by Vic Sarin, maybe Canada's most honoured cinematographer... Sarin's subtly-lit camera work has the texture and shades of a Caravaggio painting."

— Ted Shaw, *The Windsor Star*

eyepiece

ADVENTURES IN CANADIAN
FILM AND TELEVISION

VIC SARIN

eyepiece

ADVENTURES IN CANADIAN
FILM AND TELEVISION

VIC SARIN

Durvile Publications Ltd.

Calgary, Alberta, Canada
www.durvile.com
Copyright © 2017 Durvile Publications Ltd.

NATIONAL LIBRARY OF CANADA
CATALOGUING IN PUBLICATIONS DATA
Sarin, Victor 1945 -

EYEPIECE: Adventures in Canadian Film and Television
Issued in print and electronic formats
ISBN: 978-1-988824-02-4 (print pbk) ISBN:978-1-988824-08-6 (epub)
ISBN: 978-1-988824-09-3 (audiobook)

1. Biography
2. Canadian Film
3. Film Industry

I. Sarin, Vic

Book Three in the Reflections Series.
Transcribed and Edited by Lorene Shyba.

We would like to acknowledge the support of the
Alberta Government through the Alberta Book Fund.

We extend gratitude to Sunny Mohajer, Lorraine McVean, and David Bunnell.

Printed by Houghton Boston Printing, Saskatoon, Saskatchewan

Durvile is a member of the Book Publishers Association of Alberta (BPAA)
and the Association of Canadian Publishers (ACP).

First edition, first printing. 2017
Front cover photo by Noel Archambault | Back cover photo from the collection of Rt. Hon. Adrienne Clarkson
Photos within the book are from Mr. Vic Sarin's collection, unless otherwise indicated.

Dedicated to

My Children

Tobias Nicola Sarin,
Maya Liv Sarin,
Jasmine Sky Sarin, and
Jaden Rain Sarin

CONTENTS

Foreword

The Right Honourable
Adrienne Clarkson

VIC SARIN AND I GO BACK A LONG WAY! I think we probably met one of the first days I ever worked in Studio 6 on Jarvis Street in Toronto in 1965-66. I was very fortunate to break into the business in an extremely surprising way: I had no training whatsoever, never thought I would be in television, walked into a television studio, and got a job immediately.

Things like that don't happen today and I guess I look back on that and am amazed that I was able to do it. Television was so relatively young (it had begun in Canada in 1952), and there wasn't such a thing as training in journalism schools for it. I walked in with an almost-finished PhD in English literature and there I was, reviewing books on *Take 30* and — six months later — hosting the show, which lasted for me for ten years.

I do remember that one of the first times I was in studio — and I have to stay that I loved studio; big, dark, and with lighting that could be trained on specific things, rather like a metaphor for life. I walked in and I knew what the three cameras would do and I felt I knew what the camera wanted from me.

Little-known to me at the time, one of the cameramen was Vic Sarin. I do remember on one occasion very early in my career when he stepped out from behind the camera and introduced himself by making a comment about something I had said. I noticed him immediately, of course, as he was handsome in an elegant and understated way, and because his eyes shone with intelligence.

I realized later that the eyes actually shone because they saw everything in front of them. Vic is, above all, the most visual person and that's why he's become the great cameraman that he is. He receives everything visually and he can translate things into visuals for anyone who is working with him or directing him. We worked together in studio on *Take 30* from 1966 on, and when film became part of our repertoire I worked with him on film in *the fifth estate.* We often had occasion to travel together, and every time I saw him looking out the window of a car or looking over my shoulder when he was setting up a shot I knew he was seeing something that I couldn't see.

And that is the essence of the great cameraman. You think you are looking at something and you actually do not see it until you see it in the lens of the camera, which is operated by somebody who really knows how to do it.

Vic always seemed to me to be somebody who knew what he was doing and who could capture — in his use of his restricted vocabulary — the essence of what he wanted. He was always soft-spoken, polite, but firm. Vic has no "temperament" in the show business sense, but I always respected and understood that his vision was unique and that he would make everything look better than you could even possibly imagine.

We shared so many adventures together: travelling around the world in ninety-six hours to film the introduction to one of my series was only one of them.

Other times we spent longer periods together — sometimes weeks — as when we went to Iran to interview the Shah. There, we travelled all over this extraordinary country and were able to interview the Shah in his summer palace Sa'dabad. I always trusted Vic to be able to get the right shots at the right time with the least fuss. There was nothing like Vic's abilities.

One of the last times we worked together was when I took him to Italy to film *Artemisia,* my drama-documentary about the greatest woman painter of the 17th Century: Artemisia Gentileschi. Vic was sensitive to the atmosphere and he understood that it was going to be aesthetically the most important thing that I had ever done. I am enormously grateful to him for this experience and the time we spent together then.

Over a period of nearly twenty years, Vic and I worked closely together. I can say that he was one of my most valued comrade-in-arms. Television and film are collaborative efforts, and if everyone working on them is an artist, the result can be sensational. I had a number of sensational moments. Vic Sarin was always a part of them.

— The Right Honourable Adrienne Clarkson
26th Governor General of Canada (1999-2005).

Enjoyed a happy and fulfilling thirty-year career as a journalist and producer at CBC Television.

PART ONE

An

Auspicious Start

& CBC

Chapter 1

Passage to Canada

WHEN I WAS ABOUT FIFTEEN YEARS OLD IN INDIA and still known as Vijay Sarin, I was a lazy student. My parents were keen to get me thinking seriously about my studies but instead of having an interest in reading, science, and mathematics, I preferred singing, dancing or generally jumping around. At that point in life, my parents were worried that I wasn't going to make anything of myself so they sent me off for an interview with the Indian army.

Competition between relatives is common in India and my studious cousin was a point of comparison for my embarrassed parents. At the time in the mid 1950s, the British had just left India and the country's army training was still modelled after the British system, specifically Sandhurst Academy. Training consisted of a selective entry process, and four years of intense training at the National Defence Academy in Poona would result in graduation as a commissioned officer with a degree. Needless to say, it was a prestigious endeavour. My cousin, who was very well respected and loved in the family, was aiming for the same goal.

The selection process was long and competitive; out of about 5,000 candidates, there were only about 150 spots. I passed the written exam, barely, and then there was a week of intense interviews, mostly consisting of psychological tests. In one of the tests, they showed me a picture of a man with a gun that he was aiming toward another man, who was only visible in

My family: Clockwise from lower left, my mother, Prem Lata;
Vijay Sarin (me); my uncle Rup Lal, my father, Dharam Vir;
Aunt Margaret, and in the centre, my brother Vimal. 1955.

silhouette. The interviewing psychologist said, "Write what you think is happening here," so I wrote that the man had a toy gun and was just playing around with it, and the mysterious man in silhouette was simply smiling and having a good time. The psychologist asked me why I thought it was a toy gun and I replied, "Because the man in silhouette is smiling." Taken aback by my response, the psychologist challenged this notion and asked my reasoning since, as he pointed out, you can't see the man in the

My National Defence Academy recruitment class.
I am in bib number lucky 13.

dark and his expression. I answered, "That's exactly my point! We can't see his face so he could be smiling for all we know!" This was a surprise to the army psychologist because it was a different perspective than what he had been hearing before.

Looking back, it's intriguing that although I did not fully grasp this at the time, I was conscious of light and its sources from very early stages of my life. I still love the way natural light shifts all the time over twenty-four hours; how it shadow-shifts, colour-shifts, tone-shifts, and how light bounces and plays across people's faces, especially when seen through the eyepiece of a camera. Although I did not understand it deeply when I was a kid in the army recruitment office, I was fascinated by light and how the picture of a guy in silhouette could give me such a strong, but unusual, emotion. Backlit silhouette like in a sunrise, or lit from the side, or from the front; they all bring different emotions and interpretations.

In the end, I did get selected to join the army. My cousin did not. The competition was over. My family was delighted with my

*Our cricket team in Melbourne, Australia.
I am second from left in the front row. 1959.*

newfound respect and admiration amongst relatives and with the prospects of their son being somebody they could be proud of. However, my lack of interest in that career path remained. I had no intention of joining the army, despite my parents' wishes.

They encouraged me to reconsider my decision, and to understand that joining the National Defence Academy would be a wonderful career opportunity that I would regret turning down later in life. Despite the honour of being one of the 150 people to be selected out of the 5,000 applicants, I was still sure that it was not what I wanted to do with my life. Although there was never intense pressure from my parents, my decision brought them a slight sense of disappointment.

Luckily, my father, who had recently joined the External Affairs Department in the Indian Government, was soon thereafter posted to Australia as a diplomat. At the time, Australia was number one in cricket amongst the Commonwealth countries and as a big fan of cricket, I was delighted to join them on this adventure to a new country.

Our band: Tony Chan, John Cheung, and me on guitar. 1960.

Simon Bracegirdle, Ted Rose, and Virginia.
Looks like I am playing claves here. 1960.

*With my Bolex camera, along with
my friend Graham in Melbourne. 1963.*

Australia

At the time we arrived in the 1950s, the capital of Australia, Canberra, was just a small place, especially compared to the bustle of India. There was not much to do then in Canberra, especially for the younger crowd. With the insistence of my parents, I decided to attend University of Melbourne. This meant I had to leave home at a young age. My mother said to me, as I now recall it, "I want to tell you something. I have no idea what lies ahead in your life. You might end up a bad guy. You might end up being someone very famous. I don't know. But one thing I do know is that you are my son and I am your mother. And no matter what, I will always love you." The unconditional love that my mother showed me so clearly has stayed with me my entire life. My mother's words were the guiding light in my uncertain path. I never felt alone or afraid, no matter where I was or what situation I was in. Although we were very close as a family, I never returned home.

When I arrived in Melbourne, I struggled. I did not speak

*On the ABC set with my mates Andrew and David
and a much bigger camera.*

English very well and I did not like university. At the time, television had just come to Australia and I found it fascinating. It was pure magic! As soon as I saw it, I knew I wanted to be a part of this visual media. I told my parents that I did not want to go to university. Frustrated, my dad asked me, "Do you want to be a bum for the rest of your life?" I said, "No, I want to make films." After a long pause, he said, "If that's what you want to do with your life then you should do it!" I felt blessed. I understood then how wonderful my parents truly were. For that time period, with our cultural background, it was truly extraordinary how supportive my parents were of my uncommon love of visual media. They told me, "Follow your heart. No matter what it is you want to do, be good at it."

So I went off, in pursuit of that. I took a job in the local tourist office, working 9 to 5, then I played cricket right after work until it was time to go to school from 6:30 to 9:30. I had joined the Royal Technical College to study electronics, my days were always packed, and I loved every moment of it.

The Broadcast Operators Course was a two-year program, focusing on electronics related to TV and radio. As evidenced by my story about the Indian army, I was never enthusiastic about books and studying. What worked for me in this program was how visual and hands-on it was. We were often examining and discovering the world of electronics, which was foreign and mysterious to me, but something I did well at.

At the time, there was hardly anyone from my cultural background in Melbourne. The Australian Government favoured European immigrants, so I stood out, and actually enjoyed that uniqueness. I was approached often and asked questions about Indian culture and beliefs – questions like, "Why do Hindus consider cows holy?" or "Why do Indians bathe in the Ganges?" or "Are you a snake-charmer too?" Interestingly, I had to learn more about my culture to be able to answer their questions. I was very happy to share facts about my Indian homeland.

Socially, my time as a teenager in Australia was the best time I've ever had in my life but I was teased about my name, Vijay. Aussies had a difficult time pronouncing my name and they'd ask "What does it bloody mean, mate?" I told them it translated to 'Victor' and they said, "Great, that's what we're gonna call you from now on, alright?"

It was the sixties by then and it was a glorious time for music, dancing, drugs, and free love. I used to play in a little band; it attracted the girls, there were parties every night, and we had a fun time. The weekends were full of invites to various family events with friends who were eager to learn more about India. I was a novelty.

My eighteenth birthday was coming up and my father asked me what I would like. "How about a camera," I said, not knowing what else to ask for. He went to the local camera store and asked the man the best kind of camera to give a teen aged boy and the fellow said, "Ah mate, give him a movie camera. A big one." So my father bought a 16 mm Swiss Bolex camera, sent it off to me, and I received it for my birthday, along with two 100-foot-long rolls of black and white Kodak film, plus film exposure instructions.

I pretended this Triumph was my car, to impress the girls.
I actually drove a Volkswagen. Sydney Australia. 1963.

The Australian Broadcast Corporation

Two years later, I received my diploma. I was fortunate enough to be hired at the Australian Broadcast Corporation (ABC) in Sydney soon after, as a technician's assistant and was given the opportunity to do camera and sound in the studios. At the time, being a film cameraman was a prestigious job. Since TV had just come to Australia, there was hardly anyone with film experience in that country, so the film cameramen at ABC had come from England. As such, their profession incited a sense of eliteness.

Barry White, my best friend at the time, worked as a driver for the ABC, driving the cameramen and news reporters. Just shortly after I had gotten my Bolex for my birthday, there was a bushfire not too far away and Barry couldn't find a cameraman to take out to shoot news about the fire. I lived right across the highway from the ABC station so Barry told his news bosses that I had a camera, and that he knew where to find me. The producer gave him the green light and Barry drove up to my place and said, "Come on Vic, let's go and shoot this fire." I told him I'd hardly even taken the camera out of the box and didn't know how to use it yet but he insisted, saying, "Come on, you can figure it out." We took off for the bush but a few girls and some drinks came our way and we forgot about getting the story. Then at about 3 a.m., Barry came to his senses, called me an SOB, blamed me for distracting him, and said it was my entire fault if he got fired from the job. Then he gave me a shove and said "Get up! Let's get out there and see if that fire is still burning."

By the time we got there, the fire was out and the sun was coming up; there was just a little smouldering here and there. I put film in the camera – and this sounds stupid now but I was just young – I lit a small tree on fire and I took some close-up shots of the burning tree, backlit in the sunrise. I took some fairly wide shots of the smoke drifting against the morning sky and did close-up shots of the ants crawling in the dry ground. There were shots of burnt leaves drifting in the wind. It looked artsy.

I let Barry take the roll of film to ABC, mainly because I knew they would process it for free. When he got back to the studio, he was in trouble. However, he convinced them to look at my film anyway. *The Evening News* lineup editor was very impressed with what I had done. It was different than the regular format of filming as shot by other cameramen in the past. Although I had no training, I still managed to capture their attention. Through pure luck, I had caught the poetic side of the aftermath of the fires. It worked very well and Barry was asked to bring me in. To my surprise, the news clip went on the air that evening. It was exhilarating to watch what I had done on TV; I could not believe what I had managed to capture – it felt magical. That was the beginning of my adventures with the 16 mm Bolex.

The reason this worked out for me so well was the fact we were in Australia, and the news department was a wide-open frontier. Since I had no training, I was not bogged down with the European or English sensibilities, so I worked entirely from instinct, as I had no do's and don'ts of the film world. At the time, the atmosphere was '*gung-ho*' and I used to, for example, run and throw the camera up in the air because I was sure it would give us some interesting footage. I'd put the camera down on the floor and push it along with my foot, or put a plastic bag on a camera with a plastic clasp and put it under water. The Aussies loved it, "Good on ya mate, that's bloody good," they'd say.

The *ABC Weekend News* assignment editor, Kurt Laughlin, was a Canadian who was very kind to me. Every weekend, he would give me two or three assignments to earn extra cash. He planted the idea of moving to Canada in my head, telling me that Canada was a great country for freelance camera work. I had seen photos that my mother had taken back in the fifties from her trip to Banff and Jasper, Alberta and I was fascinated. The endless snow against the deep-blue skies, enormous lakes, pine trees, and the wide-open spaces. I never liked the heat of the Indian subcontinent so I remember thinking, *Wow, that's where I want to go.*

A complicating factor was that I could not stay in Australia for long due to its immigration policy. Soon after, my father's post in Australia was finished and I had the choice to either accompany my father to his next post in hot and humid Bangladesh or move to a snow-covered paradise. I chose Canada.

Canada in 1963

I got my visa to come to Canada in 1963, courtesy of my father's efforts with the Canadian High Commission in Canberra. I bought a ticket and without knowing anyone in Canada at all, landed at the small shed of an airport in cold and rainy Vancouver, which was nothing but a sleepy little town at that time. I had about two thousand Canadian dollars with me, which was enough, but I didn't know it was enough. I really had no idea about what living in Canada would cost. I was worried about what I was going to do since I didn't have a job and didn't know anybody in Canada. When I arrived at the immigration counter at the airport, the officer saw that I was coming in as an immigrant and asked, "What's your address in Canada." I told him I didn't know because I had never been here before. He said, "Well, you've got to have an address because we have to send you for a medical and send you papers. We must know your address." He was adamant.

I must tell you, I was crying inside because I didn't know what to do. I was worrying about getting back to Australia or joining my family in Bangladesh by this point, wondering if I had enough money and feeling really down about these rules I didn't know about. I went back into the airport building and started thumbing through the phone directory to find numbers for airline companies to book a trip back to Australia and that's when I saw addresses and phone numbers for residents of Vancouver. I went eenie, meenie, miney, mo and found an address and phone number for a 'Mrs. Campbell', took it to the customs officer and he accepted my story that I had remembered someone I knew. Then, he let me into Canada.

Once outside the immigration building I made a call to Mrs. Campbell, knowing that this woman would no doubt be getting official correspondence for me. An older voice answered the phone and I politely explained to her what had happened. Then I heard her say, very calmly, "All-right, Oh-kay." And that was it; the extent of my first conversation with a woman who was, in essence, my immigration sponsor.

I went to both the Vancouver CBC and CTV stations and left them my resumes but since there were no guarantees and each day was costing me money, I panicked and jumped on a train heading east. I was somewhere between Winnipeg and Toronto when I got a cable from Mrs. Campbell saying that I had a job offer from the CTV affiliate, 'Channel 8'. How she found me, to this day I truly do not know. Sending a cable used to be a big thing, expensive and troublesome and I was very moved by this kind gesture from a person who knew nothing about me.

When I got to Union Station in Toronto, I located the pay phone which meant finding mitts-full of change for long distance dialling. I then called my Channel 8 contact in Vancouver from over half way across the country and he said gruffly, "You can start tomorrow." I obviously had to reply, "I can't start tomorrow, I am in Toronto," and I explained that since I hadn't known when or even if I would hear from him, I thought I would see Canada. He told me to book a flight and get there right away.

Since I was conscious of my money situation and didn't want to pay for an airplane ticket without knowing the exact payoff, I did something I had never done before and I asked him, "Could you please tell me sir, what will my wages be?" He told me he would double what I was earning at ABC but as the conversation proceeded, I realized that when I had told him fifteen pounds, he thought I was quoting a per-month wage, when in fact it was what I had been earning per week at ABC. When I pointed out to him that accepting his offer would cut my salary in half, he wouldn't budge with the amount, so I said, "Thank you sir, but I think I'll pass."

Inside, I was dying because I had one bird in my hand and I was letting it go. I had no guarantees that I would find anything in Toronto, and I was scared to death. I checked into the Asian Hotel on Bay and Dundas Street and sat in a cold room with a bare light bulb, thinking about how I wanted to go home to Australia. But my father had accepted the posting in Bangladesh and I had no choice but to stay in Canada and try to tough it out.

To CLOSE THIS CHAPTER, I would just like to say a few words about my cherished Mrs. Campbell. I was drawn very closely to her by the kind gestures she'd made; from the cable she sent informing me of the job interview, to the very act of being my *ad hoc* immigration sponsor and contact person. For the first months that I was in Toronto, she would mail me my immigration documents and SIN application correspondence and such. I knew she was a fine human being, taking the trouble as she did, and that has stayed with me.

At CBC, we had our own private long-distance lines for news and call-in shows so I kept in touch with Mrs. Campbell that way, letting her know that I was doing well and how much I appreciated the help. She would also call me from time to time. I could tell by her voice on the phone that she was an older woman and she became like my family, almost like my mother. I had no other family in Canada at that time and I had a longing to meet her and thank her but I didn't have the money or time to go to Vancouver. In the back of my mind, though, I was always hoping to see Mrs. Campbell.

In 1966, about three years after my arrival in Toronto, I was finally assigned with a crew to go to Vancouver. I was an assistant cameraman at the time and I remember checking into the Bayshore Inn, which was, at the time, on the outskirts of Vancouver. The rest of the guys hit a bar right away but I told them I had to go see someone and would be back soon. I hopped into the rented car and headed over to an address near Broadway and Granville, to see Mrs. Campbell. I knocked on the door and there was no answer. A fellow from down the road spotted me – you have to remember that back then it was not common to see a person with brown skin colour and long curly hair in Vancouver. He came over and asked if he could help me and I said, "Yes, I am looking to see if Mrs. Campbell is home," and he said, "Well, lad, you are a little too late. She passed away not long ago."

I went back to my car and choked up a little. I'd never met Mrs. Campbell but she was a guardian angel to me and, for all that time, my surrogate mother. I never saw her or met her and yet I felt that I knew her so well. My introduction to Canada was the kindness of a total stranger. Small things can stay with you all your life, but in a bigger sense, I remain to this day very taken with Canada and how kind people are.

Colour

Plates

*My father, Dharam Vir, my mother Prem Lata and me
in Kashmir, India, 1947.*

*With my close Australian friends Janet Frost and Mary Grey,
who came to visit me in Canada, 1965.*

Filming dog tricks on an early documentary about Wilbur Plauger the legendary American rodeo clown. 1964.

Naked Peacock *was a documentary I with with Dennis Hargreaves that featured nudism at various nudist camps across America. 1975*

I travelled with Pierre Burton for several weeks on
The National Dream. *I asked him to sit on the tracks, and he did. 1974*

Our National Dream *team*
profiled against The National Dream steam engine. 1974.

With Ron Neely, host of Country Canada, *in Egypt on a three-hour special we did on food and population. 1972.*

With Donald Sutherland on Bethune. *He was so committed, he got very thin for this role. 1977.*

Behind the camera (far right), shooting Queen Elizabeth and Prince Philip at Rideau Hall, chatting with Madame Pauline Vanier. 1977.

In Finland with director Alan King and actor Boot Savage on the film The Last Season. *1986.*

Dancing with villagers during our location shoot of Falashas, *about Ethiopian Jews. 1983.*

In Iran with Louise Lore, who was executive producer of Man Alive. *We were dressed up as Persians.*

*Prime Minister Pierre Trudeau being consulted on a script
by the producer and journalist Jeannine Locke.*

*Rebecca Jenkins looking dubiously at the elephant's tusks
on the set of* Bye Bye Blues. *1987.*

With Indira Gandhi who I had the great pleasure of interviewing, along with a Canadian scholar.

With Suzanne Cook in Kathmandu, Nepal for Solitary Journey. *1989.*

Dalai Lama was tending his garden and as he was doing so I took this shot. His kind, gentle soul is a great and cherished memory in my life. 1982.

Helena Bonham Carter on the
Margaret's Museum *shoot. 1995*

Out on the water with Margaret's Museum *actors*
Clive Russell and Helena Bonham Carter. 1995.

Trial at Fortitude Bay *with actors*
Robert Ito and Lolita Davidovich. 1994.

Robert Richard and Lou Gessett Jr. on
set of In His Father's Shoes. *1997*

*With Tina Pehme at the time we were
working on* Partition. *2006.*

*Sharing some ideas with Jimi Mistry and
Neve Campbell on* Partition.

On the set of A Shine of Rainbows *schoolroom,*
with Connie Neilsen. 2008.

In India during the shooting of Hue. *2013.*

In Namibia, scouting locations. 2015

At the home in France of cinematographer
Philippe Rousselot. 2016.

At the home in Italy of cinematographer
Vittorio Storaro. 2016.

Diane and Tobias Sarin in Ontario in 1971.

The family at Maya Sarin's graduation in San Diego.
Left to right: Jaden, Tina, Jasmine, Maya, and me. 2016.

Chapter 2

Early Television Days at CBC

I JOINED CBC ON THE FATEFUL DAY of November 22, 1963. The director of programming and technical services at that time, Reg Horton, was looking at my aptitude test results when news was whispered in his ear that John F. Kennedy had just been shot. Reg was understandably distracted so he looked at me and simply said; "Well, what are you waiting for?" and I said, "Sir, I am just waiting to get employment here." "You're hired," he said. "You start tomorrow." And there was it. I thank President Kennedy, in a very sad way, for helping me acquire my job at CBC, thus launching my adventures in the world of Canadian television.

Television

I started out by working in Kine Recording as a film processor technician but soon I got a break to go work in the studio, and I was absolutely delighted. It gave me a chance to get behind the television studio camera, although I longed to be in the film department. The show was *The Friendly Giant*, which was a kids program featuring Robert Homme, along with hand puppets Rusty the Rooster and Jerome the Giraffe. The signature shot for the show started with the camera on a dolly from a very wide shot, moving towards the castle drawbridge. Once the camera was at the drawbridge, they'd cut inside to Bob who was the host for the show.

In those days the camera bodies were massively bulky and

CBC Still Photo Collection

Pulling the camera in toward The Friendly Giant's castle.
"I'll go on ahead and lower the drawbridge. Here's my castle"

we used to go live to air quite often. So on the dolly shot towards the drawbridge, we used a 'long-lens' in order to fill the frame with the drawbridge at the end of the dolly push. The camera body had to be at a distance from the drawbridge so as not to create any shadows with the overhanging lights. As everyone in the industry knows, the longer the lens, the more critical the focus so if you move two or three inches in the wrong direction, the focus falls apart. In order to dolly in, I'd have to stay in focus with one hand on the camera while pushing the camera in toward the shot with the other. These were huge cameras and I am not a big guy. Talk about a challenge.

Live television was often nerve wracking but I thrived on the adrenaline. With live TV, your focus is totally in the moment and you cannot become distracted. I really enjoyed the big rush of it. After a half-hour show, all the boys on the cameras would be drenched with sweat, even in winter. It was the nerves. You knew

University of Wisconsin-Madison Archives

The Friendly Giant, Bob Homme amidst our low-tech special effects in the studio, circa 1968.

that if you made a mistake, it had already gone out on the air and millions had already watched it. Looking back, I'd say that doing live television made me trust and commit to what I saw through the lens, and it also gave me a sense of pride and responsibility.

While I was waiting for my big break to get into the Film Department, I worked on a number of other early CBC shows such as *This Hour has Seven Days, Front Page Challenge, This*

Land, Take 30, News Magazine, Mr. Dressup, Razzle Dazzle, Variety Specials, and *Wayne and Schuster.* I recall that Juliette Cavazzi, who was "Our Pet Juliette" in *The Juliette Show,* was a real stickler about being shot from certain angles that she thought to be flattering. By working on these shows in the studio, I got a spectrum of what CBC was doing across the board.

The Only Game in Town

In the 1960s, CBC television enjoyed the best success of any Canadian network at that time and the reason was simple; it was the only network around – there was nothing else really happening. Granted, after 1961 there was CTV and they were doing daily news and public affairs shows, but mostly CTV was screening American programs. But CBC was the only platform for Canadian shows. We did dramas, variety specials, outdoor events, documentaries and news – CBC had a mandate to care for the full cross-section of our society, whatever the needs. *Country Canada* had maybe only 100,000 viewers but CBC looked after the needs of rural folks; after all they were taxpayers so they deserved it. We did a variety of shows catering to all kinds of Canadians, which was fantastic because this gave Canadians a much broader sense of the country and the culture. I admire how such a huge country with four time zones, harsh weather, two official languages, and multiple cultures was able to come together. CBC played a huge role in uniting Canada.

Although I'd worked for the Australian Broadcast Corporation before coming to Canada, CBC was kind of a step up for me because CBC was in a bigger country and had a bigger budget. In my mind, I had escalated to the next level. In an emotional sense, I felt pretty good about that. In those days, CBC television was enjoying a tremendous and spirited success. There was a show called *This Hour has Seven Days* that pioneered ways to find the truth behind each story they covered. That's the only show for which the whole country would almost stop whatever they were doing to watch. It was exciting because I had never seen such a thing before. The American program *60 Minutes* was based on the format that *This Hour* had pioneered.

CBC Still Photo Collection

*Juliette Cavazzi, "Our Pet Juliette" who was keen
to be shot from particular angles.*

CBC Still Photo Collection

*Panelists including Gordon Sinclair, Betty Kennedy, and Pierre Burton
on* Front Page Challenge, *with a mystery guest.*

CBC Still Photo Collection

Patrick Watson and Laurier LaPierre, ground-breakers in Canadian journalism on This Hour Has Seven Days.

We also had other news magazine shows that were very well respected. We had Tuesday night documentary shows, we had *Take 30* with Adrienne Clarkson, who had joined the world of television, and *Front Page Challenge* with Pierre Burton and the gang. It was a time when we saw a strong variety of programs, all with very Canadian values. There was no NBC, ABC, or CBS because there was no cable or licensing – nothing like that. We'd get shows from BBC once and a while, but basically we did our own thing. So in one sense, we developed not only our own sensibilities, but also a way to fill the needs of what we liked as Canadians, our own taste. That said, one cannot ignore certain voices within the country who were critical of CBC's slow pace and the 'look' of the show – especially the lighting.

By way of a funny story from those days, I had long black hair and was often teased about my looks – I suppose I looked like a biblical character. One particular cameraman, Bill Poulious, took to staring at me, sizing me up, I guess. One day I said to

*Paul Soles, Jehane Benoît, and Adrienne Clarkson
on set for a cooking segment of* Take 30.

him, "Bill, what's wrong?" and he said, "Vic, you should be an actor." He would bug me about this once and a while and finally my ego got the better of me and I started thinking, *Hey maybe I could be an actor*. So I told him, "Bill, I am very self-conscious about the way I speak English," and he reassured me saying, "Don't worry about it. You'll be just fine."

I agreed but still wanted to see the script for the production, but he wouldn't give it to me. As the time of production grew nearer, I became more concerned, mostly because of my English, but he still wouldn't show me the script. Finally the day arrived and he gave me the address and directions and continued to press me to just trust him and that everything would be fine. When I got there, my role was to play Jesus Christ on the Cross! That was my big break as an actor.

THE FILM DEPARTMENT at CBC, that I had hoped to be part of from my very first interview, was a small but elite entity within the CBC. People who worked in film felt they were a little bit better than the television crowd. There were two sides of producing shows at CBC; one was done on tape with television cameras, the other was done on film. I still wanted to get into film, firstly because I had been shooting for ABC News in Australia and had fallen in love with film right from there and secondly, electronically, I was not really trained for the technical side of television and besides that, it was not exactly my cup of tea.

Film was a much more independent part of the business. One had the chance to go out on locations, travel a good deal of the time, and experience different cultures and different places. The biggest drawing card about film for me was the independence plus the personal control; you had your camera and yourself and that was it. There was no 'Take Two'. These things were not an option in television those days where you had a big heavy camera, big crews and tons of people, so I was longing to go to the Film Department.

Working the News

I worked for two years for CBC's news department in 1968 and 1969, covering stories locally, nationally and internationally. I am grateful because as I look back it, was excellent training. I worked closely with News Department heads such as William Cunningham, as well as with Joe Schlesinger, Peter C. Newman, and other great reporters such as Gordon Stewart, Jeff Hussey, and Terry Hargreaves. As I look back, I admire these strong individuals and the only thing they cared about was the news. They didn't need to care about the budgets or the scheduling – for them it was just, "Get the goddamn news."

I remember once saying *good morning* to Bill Cunningham and as an aside I said to him, "Did you hear about the kids in Mexico? They are rebelling about something." Bill looked at me and said, "Well, what are you doing then?" I said "What do you mean 'what am I doing?', I am just telling you the story that is happening there." He shouted at me, "Get travel arrangements done by the unit manager and get your ass down to Mexico, shoot, and if there is something good, we will send a reporter."

*John Lennon and Yoko Ono on their way
to Montreal for the* Give Peace a Chance *bed-in.*

Wow, I thought. I'm just a camera guy, just a nobody.

I wasn't a writer or a reporter but Bill was totally open, no bureaucracy, no bullshit, and believed strongly in the visuals for the story. Bill's attitude was always, "Go get the story." Now you have to ask ten places just to get something done instead of acting independently. I had no rules or constraints about anything when it came to the camera, so the news reporters loved me. Most of the other camera guys were pretty stuffy in those days because they would get all worried about focus or tripping over something, but I didn't care, I would do anything I wanted and I had no fear of any technicalities.

John and Yoko (1969)

John Lennon and Yoko Ono came to Toronto in 1969, heading to their famous Give Peace a Chance sleepover they had in Montreal. My news assignment editor sent me out to get some footage for *The National* that night so I went out to Malton Airport with the sound man – standard stuff because we covered news stories every day. John was having a difficult time at Canada Immigration because he was still dealing with some marijuana-related charges – in fact that was why he was in Canada at all. John wasn't allowed in the US. When he landed, he'd been herded off to an immigration hearing and I stood waiting outside the small room with the rest of the media – CTV, *Toronto Star, Globe and Mail* – we were all there. I had a heavy film news camera and was all strapped up with my heavy battery belts and all kinds of other cables and gadgets.

Since I am a not a big guy, I used to often squat down and shoot through the legs of the big strapping camera guys from the other networks who'd be scuffling to get their cameras up close to the action. But this time, John exited the small immigration room and immediately began walking briskly down a narrow corridor, so I had to scramble up and compete in the tight space with the others to walk along with him. I decided that since there was no room, I would sprint out in front and walk backwards, which is pretty foolhardy, considering I couldn't see what was behind me. Normally the sound man would keep an eye out for me in tricky situations like that, but since there was such a big scrum of reporters there, he was having a hard time just holding his microphone in the jostling crowd.

After only about fifteen seconds of backwards walking, I hit a railing by the staircase and as the footage that I shot attests, just before my camera went flying out of my arms, you can see John for a few frames reaching out for me and saying, "Are you alright mate? You okay?" Then a couple of hours later, he had a second hearing and guess what. Same thing again. I was walking backwards and this time I hit the rail with my back and tumbled on the landing, narrowly avoiding a fall down the concrete staircase. John came and picked me up and I remember him saying, "We can't keep you off the ground can we?" Almost like saying to me *hey, what's the next trick you are going to do?* After that, he got his permission to land.

I realize that this was a ridiculous, maybe even humiliating way to endear yourself to somebody, but the sound guy and I ended up in the first-class section of a flight to Montreal with

John and Yoko. On the one-hour flight, Yoko was warm but very quiet. In contrast, John was very excited and bright, but with his thick Liverpool accent and the way he talked in riddles, I must admit, I didn't follow everything he said. What I do remember is that he talked about his recent experience with Maharishi Mahesh Yogi at an ashram in India. I let him know how much his music meant to me, and John remained animated, talkative and very warm. I felt that the friendly connection we had was partly because of my love for his music, but also partly because I am Indian and that the Beatles had just returned from there.

The sad part of the story is that at the end of the flight, he invited me to come to the Montreal sleepover and film it. Like a stupid fool, I said I had to get back to Toronto to get the story on the news. I should have said *"Absolutely!"* and sent the film back by courier or something. I missed out on one of the greatest events of the century and could have sung or at least hummed along to *Give Peace a Chance* with John and Yoko, and other legends like Timothy Leary, Allen Ginsberg, and Tommy Smothers. What an idiot I was to miss that chance!

The Middle East

In about 1970 a Middle-East war broke out between the Jordanians and the PLO *fedayeen*. I was assigned to go over with Bill Cunningham who had just come back from Vietnam where he had a reputation for being a tough war correspondent. We flew to Lebanon and spent ten days there and he wouldn't let me go out to the front. He said to me, "No, no that's not our story, we're going to wait." Meanwhile I was all *gung-ho* and had hired local taxi driver and because of my ethnic background I said, "I can sneak in because they won't even know I'm a foreigner." But Bill protected me. He said, "Vic, you know it's not important enough to die for." So we didn't do anything. I give credit to Bill for identifying that the story of interest to us was not about homeland bickering, it was about what the PLO was doing to the outside world. "Unless we get that story, " Bill told me, "why take a chance." Of course he had been through it all before with his various war postings.

With our 'fixer' amidst the crowd in Cairo in 1970,
covering Gamal Abdul Nasser's funeral.

Just about then, Egyptian president Gamal Abdul Nasser died and CBC sent me from Lebanon to Cairo to cover his funeral. CBC Correspondent David Halton flew in from Toronto and joined me there, as he was CBC's Middle East correspondent at the time. On the day that Nasser's body was taken to the burial ground, I was one of the many media people shooting footage of the gun carriage with his body passing along the bridge over the Nile. What was about to transpire was the closest I ever came to getting killed in my entire career.

When the crowd saw the gun carriage carrying the body of Nasser across the bridge over the Nile, they lost control getting very emotional, and rushed straight at us. In the intense crush of thousands of people stampeding across the bridge, I got clobbered and went flying, along with my camera and the small box I used to stand on and which carried my spare camera and film. I passed out and all I know is that my camera saved me because the locals could see that I was a foreigner. But my small box was gone and along with it with the story I had just shot that morning of the grief-stricken crowds. A small group of caring

*In Cairo with sound man Eddie Chong
during the time of
Nasser's funeral procession, 1970.*

gave me a little water and helped me to my feet. I made my way to the media centre and David Halton attempted to console me. I was very upset because my box was gone, the story was gone, and I'd almost lost my life.

I went to the police station to file a report of my missing box and they assured me that they would find it in no time, though I was very skeptical that they would accomplish this in a city of six million, especially at a time like this. When I got back to the hotel, a message was waiting for me to call the Canadian Embassy. The box, which had CBC's address in Canada on it, had been returned to the embassy along with a note saying that I had good taste in camera equipment and that they hoped I got everything back untouched. The people who found and returned my small box complete with the story footage made me feel intensely positive about the human race.

• • •

What I learned from working on *The National* and other CBC news programs was foundational to my career. Whether I was working with Bill Cunningham, David Halton, Terry Hargreaves, Trina McQueen, Joe Schlesinger or any other of the outstanding news professionals, technically I was able to shoot whatever I wanted to – nobody told me what to do. I was totally on my own as a cameraman, getting the visuals to communicate the essence of the story. I had to work spontaneously and instinctively, and at the same time have a sense of the story. Also, the independence encouraged me to be more responsible. It was the best training I could have had for my career. If you don't get the visuals from the onset, most often you won't get a second chance. If you try to stage it, you risk losing the honesty and purity.

Chapter 3

Early Documentaries

CBC HAS ALWAYS HAD a strong social conscience and was in the forefront of documentaries about many things, including the environment. I worked as an assistant cameraman on *The Nature of Things* special in 1969 for Larry Gosnell, who had just come over to CBC from the National Film Board and who was very concerned about the destruction of nature by mankind. The first three shows we did aimed to bring awareness to the issues of air pollution, water pollution, and pesticides. We were the first broadcasters in Canada to talk about these issues. Right after those shows were done, *Time Magazine* had a cover story on bad air. I feel that we instigated awareness of these problems with our work at CBC. We did another three-part series on population and food, which we shot around the world. The producer was Doug Louer, who was caring, humorous and very fun to work with.

We were ahead of the curve and very conscientious about events of the world. I remember rushing down to California for CBC news with reporter Larry Bondy to cover a story about Caesar Chavez, the Mexican farmworker who had organized the Farmworkers Union in California. There were, of course, no satellite or Internet uploads in 1969, so to make it work, we had to hand over the physical film. We interviewed Chavez's workers at 5:00 a.m., then, as I carried on shooting, Larry ran to the local bus station, took the bus to San Francisco, and then handed the film over to an Air Canada pilot who had a scheduled flight back to Toronto. The film was picked up in Toronto in time for processing and editing to get the story on the air on the six o'clock news. Keep in mind, there was also a three-hour time difference. It was very competitive between the news reporters and channels to get big stories on air the same night, and news reporters had to be particularly dedicated and focused. There were no gimmicks and the news gathering process was perfectly well tuned.

One of the most difficult assignments I worked on was a special one-hour film called "Coming and Going" for *The Nature of Things*. A freelance filmmaker David Cherniak had come to CBC with an idea about the recent formation of a new ward " TCU" attached to the St. Boniface Hospital in Winnipeg. The purpose for this unit was to make terminally ill patients as comfortable as possible and let them have anything they desired in the last stages of their lives. David's idea was pure and simple; let's make a film by seeing and observing the life in the ward and its patients – a day in TCU.

The subject matter was very tough for me because I felt that if I was a patient at the hospital and was wheeled into the TCU ward, I would know my days were numbered and my hope for life would be taken away - hope is what keeps us going. It was also challenging to figure out a way to weave a story out of these circumstances. Our sound man, Gerry King, rigged the rooms in the ward with wireless microphones so he didn't have to be directly on site. David Cherniak would drop in once in a while to see how things were going but, for the most part, I was on my own amid the patients. At TCU, I got to know the staff and patients quite well and I saw life in the most difficult time. I witnessed anger, remorse, love, pain and compassion; but above all, the reality of life. A few patients died while I was there. At times, I also stayed overnight in the ward.

One early morning I got summoned by the nurse informing me that Mr. Pendergast, one of my favourite patients, was slipping. It was tough news for me to hear, but my own emotions no doubt paled compared to that of his wife who was holding her dying husband's hand. As I started to film, I was overcome with all kinds of emotions but mostly guilt, asking myself, *Why I am filming at a time when I should be comforting Mrs. Pendergast? Am I exploiting the situation for my own gain?*

I felt horrible and stopped the camera to join Mrs. Pendergast and comfort her. She saw me stop filming and understood my dilemma. She encouraged me to continue filming, saying, "Vic, people need to see and feel what the honesty of life is. It is good to capture the truth." I went back and started to film again. Soon after, Mr. Pendergast took his last breath. I stayed with him for a few seconds and gently panned over to the open window next to his bed where, at the time, Christmas trees were rolling in for sale in the open courtyard below.

It is always difficult to assess when one is exploiting the situation for the camera - how one draws the line whether to film or not. It is a moral dilemma. The camera has a very strong power, and that power has to be approached with respect.

The Family Prince (1975)

We had a CBC producer in the 1970s, Jeannine Locke who could be difficult at times, but who had a deep knowledge and understanding about Canada. I admired her on many levels, not the least of which was her conscientious work ethic. She was a journalist herself – she'd come into television from *The Toronto Star* – and had strong feelings of loyalty for the British monarchy. With her journalistic background, she was a good writer but wasn't into visual filming so we clicked as a team and we worked for many years together on her documentaries. She did a special called *The Canadian Monarchy*, which I partly shot for her, and she also did one on Charles, Prince of Wales called *The Family Prince*, which I shot in its entirety.

We had interviews set up for at the Governor General's residence in Ottawa; that's where the Royal Family used to stay as guests when in Canada. Jeannine Locke was something of a nervous person, she used to smoke heavily and sometimes she would stutter a little bit, especially when she was under pressure. So that day, I knew I would have to carry some of the conversation. Something I had going for me, or against me

*Queen Elizabeth and Prince Philip in a moment of
repose during filming of* The Canadian Monarchy.

depending on how you look at it, was that I was an immigrant,
the implication being that I perhaps it looked like I didn't know
much about this country. When dealing with monarchy, you are
meant to address them in certain ways and you are meant to call
them "'Your Majesty', or 'Your Highness', – not just 'Sir'. I wasn't
very good at doing those things and I would never remember to
address people with the right protocol so I would just call them
'Sir' or 'Madam' and that was it.

So there I was, shooting Prince Charles through the lens of
the camera. Most people those days who I was shooting would
relate directly to me because I was the only one watching and
nobody else on out could see anything. Interview subjects would
often ask me, "How was I?" or "How am I doing?" So we did the
interview which was an hour or an hour-and-a-half and at the
end of the interview, as I was helping the sound guy with the
microphone, Prince Charles said to Jeannine and me, because
she was behind the camera too, "Is there anything else you
would like?" Jeannine looked at me and I had a little moment of

should I or shouldn't I but I went ahead anyway and said, "Yes Sir, if you wouldn't mind if I ask you a little favour?" I saw all the faces of his aides and bodyguards going red, as I'm sure they were thinking *Oh Hell this guy just got off the boat.*

I said to Prince Charles, "If you don't mind, please go back down the corridor, just around the corner there and walk past that camera to give me a good ten-second shot." He said "All right then," so I set the camera up and all his aides, who wanted to just whisk him away, honest to God, looked so embarrassed. Once he finished that stroll past the camera, he said to me, "How was I, was I alright?" and I said, "Would you mind if I do it one more time?" Well this time, I really thought they were going to kill me, these aides, but Prince Charles went along with me, even asking what wasn't done right last time. I said "Sir, what would be nice is if you just take your time, don't rush. As if you are thinking – you are inside of your mind." So now he understood what I was trying to get from him. I wanted to make him more human and expose his inner life. Why was I sure I could take this chance, cross these boundaries, and finish the leap in a successful way? Something I know now and knew then too is that we all want to look good and do the right thing for the camera.

Documenting Bangladesh

While I was having the time of my life at CBC experiencing other cultures and creative challenges, my parents were busy feeling sorry for me. They'd been frustrated that I hadn't wanted to come back to India so my father took an early retirement and took a position as local staff with the Indian High Commission in Ottawa so they could be close to me. They didn't really know much about what I did for a living, just that I worked for CBC and was on the 'technical side'. My mother had seen me running around with a camera a few times, and to them I was like a menial labourer all belted up with a big bulky camera, carrying heavy boxes like an 'underling', so they felt sorry for me and wished I had a better job. Because my dad was a bureaucrat, to them the successful person was the one who sits behind a desk, has a couple of assistants, and has tea brought to him in the afternoon.

In 1974 there was a famine in Bangladesh and on the nightly news we would see the cows just lying there on the dry land, children not being able to get milk from their mothers' breasts, and other sad sights. I thought, *Yes, this is a story, but why do famines happen more frequently in Bangladesh.* So I said to CBC "I want to go do a film on that." They said, "Fine if you want to, just find out who's available to assist you as your crew..." and I said, "No, I want to go alone. I want to go live with a family who is on the verge of starvation so I can get a sense of what it's like to be on the verge of starvation." CBC was a bit apprehensive but they encouraged me to do so.

So I called my father who had been posted years before as a diplomat in Bangladesh, and said, "Dad I want to go to Bangladesh to do a story on the famine there." He said "I would advise you not to go," and he went on to explain that Bangladesh used to be East Pakistan, the West Pakistanis treated East Pakistanis very poorly, and that prejudice between the groups was very strong. He pointed out that I looked much like the West Pakistanis and he was afraid for me because the Liberation war had taken place a few years before that when West Pakistan had attacked the East. My father then said, "I don't think it will be good for you to go alone," and then said, much to my surprise, "I will come with you."

It was a long flight – fifty hours to get to Bangladesh from Toronto, with delays here and there. My dad was an older man at the time, more or less the same age I am now, and so the trip tired him out. We got to Dhaka to a nice five-star hotel and while he was resting up, I went on my own and found a village where a family had been really hit hard. I went to the village and talked to the family that was having a hard time and asked them if they minded if I lived there with them and document them for a while. I told my dad that I was moving out to the village to spend time with the family and he asked, "Son, is it really necessary to do that?" I told him, "I want to make a documentary, that's what I am here for. I want to feel what it's like in the moment when there is no food." I was with the family for about ten days and in that time, my father used to come out to the village and would sneak a bit of food in for me. I'd tell him, "I'm grateful but I need to not eat and be with them until I finish the film."

From the time I moved into the village until the time we left, my father watched me quite a bit because he had nothing else to do. He had come on the trip to protect me – so nobody would hurt me – but he saw for the first time what film meant to me and what it takes to make a film. It was a small window for him to the world of filmmaking. After about the first week he'd get excited and say things like, "Remember you wanted a sunrise shot? I just saw it down the road." Or he would say "I think you wanted a shot of a cow licking a dry field, I saw it by the river." Experiencing my work opened up his eyes and he became my scout and my best fan. He never spoke about my profession and its difficulties to me again. However, it's only after his death I found out that after returning from Bangladesh, every time any films I had worked on showed on TV, he'd tell all his friends to tune in and watch his son's work. Apparently, he spoke to friends constantly about the kind of work I do and how proud he was of me.

The Shah of Iran (1976)

In 1976, one of the assignments I did with *the fifth estate* was shooting an interview with the Shah of Iran. It was a fascinating time when the Shah was in total control, and, at the same time, he was accused of having a secret police, SAVEK, reportedly torturing Iranian citizens. He was very close to the West, acquiring a new cache of Bell helicopters. It was a high profile *Fifth Estate* episode and Adrienne Clarkson was the host. Adrienne describes in her memoir, *Heart Matters*, that she clearly remembers the opulence of the Abad Palace where the interview was conducted, under the watchful eyes of the armed guards. I remember being very impressed with the Shah. When we were introduced, the Shah would stare right into our eyes and he remembered everybody's name.

It was a long and tense interview because as expected, Adrienne would point out reports that his police were using torture and he would bark right back that the newspapers were garbage. Every time he used the word "garbage" to describe the

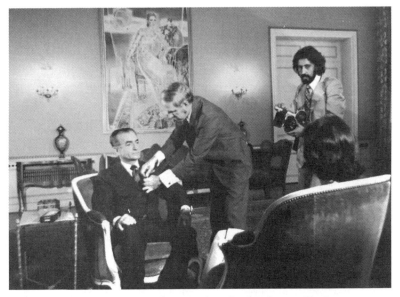

Getting set up to shoot in the Abad Palace with the Shah of Iran, Adrienne Clarkson, and Stuart French.

media, his tone of voice would get more shrill and I noticed through the viewfinder that he was starting to sweat.

Although we had only a limited amount of time to spend, the film magazines needed to be changed every ten minutes. During those changes, the Shah would avoid Adrienne and turn his attention to my camera. He was very keen to talk about the camera and its accessories; even to the point of potentially throwing us off schedule. I sensed that he was making a concerted effort to relax in those moments, possibly priming up himself mentally for Adrienne's next line of difficult questions.

At the end of the interview, the Shah asked us if there was anything else we would like. Gordon Stewart, our producer, gave a quick look at Adrienne and me and I immediately said, "Yes, it would be nice if we could follow you in the next day or two and film whatever you are doing?" There was an awkward moment when everybody was looking at each other and then the Shah looked at a security guard in the distance and then right back at us and said, "Sure. We will pick you up tomorrow at the hotel at

*With Prime Minister Indira Gandhi, in the courtyard of
her home in New Delhi, India.*

nine o'clock." At that point, we all felt being in the presence of monarchy and power.

We came to realize that was an interesting ploy on the part of the Shah of Iran. Rather than us chasing the SAVAK around and possibly uncovering their activities, by keeping us in his sight we were less of a threat. It was a smart diplomatic move to have us under his wing to keep us out of trouble. Those were the days of *the fifth estate* series when we would go out as a team and actively uncover the news and so it was something of a disappointment to me not to get the actual visual evidence of what was going on in Iran. The show became more 'talking-heads' and I have always believed, *Let's not talk, show me the evidence.*

Indira Gandhi

Throughout my career at CBC, I would find people around me making excuses for why something or other couldn't be done. I always gravitated to the opposite. I was always keen to see how we could make something work that was thought of as difficult.

In 1980 I was in India for a project, and the crew and I were stuck in New Delhi for a few days because out-bound flights were not available. I thought that since we in town for a few days, we should go talk to Mrs. Gandhi. I admired her because she was a female prime minister running a country of almost a billion people. I told Gail Carr and Ian Challis, my crew members, about my plan and they said, "Oh sure, you're just going to walk in and talk to the Prime Minister of India." Of course they were being sarcastic but I said, "Let's try anyway and see what happens."

I tried phoning to make an appointment but that was an impossible task given the phone system, so we took a taxi out to her residence in Delhi. The fact that Gail and Ian were two Europeans in India helped me to gain entry to meet Mrs. Gandhi's private secretary. I introduced myself to her as being from CBC and said that we would like to interview Prime Minister Gandhi. The secretary then asked us to request an official appointment through the Canadian High Commission. For a moment, it looked like that was it, but I gave her my pitch – that we'd found ourselves there unexpectedly for only a few days and that I was a big fan and would love to meet her. The secretary was polite but I could tell she wasn't falling for it.

Then in the background, I saw Mrs. Gandhi walk by and I sensed that she glanced our way. In the meantime the secretary was busy trying to dismiss us, saying that we should go through the proper channels. Then the secretary got summoned away and I think it was Mrs. Gandhi asking her what we were doing there at her residence. Anyway, the secretary came back and said Prime Minister Gandhi would see us the next day for half an hour at two o'clock. Although she had previously said half an hour only, we ended up spending three hours with her.

I panicked a bit, realizing that I needed someone to come along who really knew India and its politics. I got hold of a Canadian woman who was a researcher at Delhi University and we decided the interview should be a knowledge-building exercise, rather than a confrontation on about specific issues. I also saw both her sons, Sunjay and Rajiv, who came and went. Besides a guard or two being present, we were alone with her.

Gail Carr, Ian Challis, Dalai Lama, and me.
Dharamsala, India, 1982.

I could have given it to *the fifth estate* but instead I wanted to keep it to do a documentary of my own about the Nehru-Gandhi dynasty. Sadly only a few months after the interview, Sunjay Gandhi was killed in a glider crash, and Mrs. Gandhi herself was assassinated a few years later by guards in the very courtyard where we had spoken to her. Rajiv Gandhi later become Prime Minister and he too was assassinated. All three of them are now gone. The footage was never broadcast.

Dalai Lama

Buddhism fascinates me and for my entire career I have wanted to do a documentary on Buddhism. I still may. After I had visited Mrs. Gandhi, I said to Gail Carr and Ian Challis, who had been with me on that interview, "Let's go to Ladakh." So we went to Ladakh, which is like a small Tibet in India. They'd opened the road for tourists for in 1982 so I knew we would have access to that area and would be among the first visitors. When we got to there, it was absolutely amazing to me. I have never had such an experience since. The town of Leh, capital of the Ladakh region, is twelve thousand feet above sea level, up in the high mountain passes and it oozed a peaceful tranquility with gentle monks in saffron robes strolling around small monasteries. We would regularly see the Ladakhis with their prayer wheels and one could feel the spirituality of the place very strongly. I knew then that I wanted to do a film about the Buddhist Lama and Buddhist monks.

We headed down to Dharamsala which is a place just south of Leh where the Dalai Lama had been living over the years since he had been exiled from Tibet in 1959. Once again, my two friends thought trying to get an interview was a pretty crazy idea, but we went ahead anyway. Dalai Lama was, and still is by all accounts, a gracious and gentle human being.

His English wasn't very good at the time – kind of a broken English you would say – but we had a chance to sit with him for a bit and then walk through the garden. What I liked about him was that he was so 'poetic'; that is the word I would use for him. And he laughed a lot. I asked him why China wanted to take over Tibet and he said, "One time, Chinese called us six million flowers. We are very happy. Then flowers become dandelions. Then they cut you." He always spoke in metaphors and it was brilliant to me. Our conversations were full of those metaphors. He laughed with us and he presented to me as being very humble, but deep. I was honoured to be in his presence.

He and his staff were very kind to us, and I was able to shoot some visuals with him. At the time, I felt that he was a spiritual person but also very practical and conscious of everything around the world.

As we were leaving, I asked the Dalai Lama if he would ever like to go back to Tibet and he laughed and said, "Of course, of course." Then I said, "If you ever go back, can I come with you?" and he laughed again and answered, "Yes, yes you can." I cherish our unwritten promise above all else.

Chapter 4

The Film Department

I N THE SIXTIES AND SEVENTIES, CBC was scattered around in buildings all over Toronto, unlike the BBC or ABC in Australia that had big headquarters, housing all departments. By working in the various CBC studios, I got to know the organization and its personnel quite well. Over the years when I desired being in the Film Department but had to pay my dues in television, I came to understand the CBC Toronto set-up and the mandate to cater to a whole cross-section of Canadians. I also got to know a lot of the people.

The Film Department was a small, isolated department within the CBC that was well respected and well loved but on its own. I think I was the first person from my Indian ethnic background to work for CBC, and definitely the first in the Film Department. Most of the people working in film, the cameramen in particular, had come from England and, as had been the case in Australia with ABC, the Film Department was populated with people who had an air of superiority. The portability and the knowledge of the film chemistry gave a special air of confidence to the film cameramen. There was an air of prestige and mystique attached to voyaging with a camera to the deepest jungles of Africa or the coldest places in the North, shooting from a helicopters, or using an underwater housing in the water.

At first, I was surrounded by people who felt that I knew little about Western culture and that I was only a kid from backwater someplace. They didn't realize that previously I had experience at ABC, so despite being looked down upon, I had confidence in myself as being at least as well qualified as many of the existing ranks. Understandably, there were difficulties at the beginning on that level with certain people in the department who weren't happy to have me around because of my different culture. It was a very different time then, and I felt discouraged and disappointed.

I wrote to the Australian Broadcast Corporation and I got a heart-warming response from the Chairman, Sir Charles Moses, who said I was welcome to come back any time. After that positive response from Australia, I was set on leaving. However, when I spoke to my boss George Desmond, the head of the CBC Film Department, he reassured me that it would get better. So I stayed, and the irony of the whole thing is that the same people who said I was the wrong person for the job ended up being my good friends, giving me numerous accolades as well. In time, things do heal and we change our own perceptions.

I am supposed to be a technical person as a camera guy and I've shot Super 8, 16 mm, 35 mm, IMAX, 3D, and now digital cameras, but I've never stopped to learn how cameras work. Rather, the camera is just a tool to me and I'm not that interested in it technically. What I am interested in is what the camera can do for me. As long as the camera can take me where I want to go with my emotion, I'm happy with it. Many of my counterparts get bogged down with technicalities – I would hear, "Oh this lens is so sharp," or "not as sharp," or "this colour rendition is not that good." I seldom worried about those things unless there was something really blatantly wrong. To this day, I am more interested in what this tool can do for me. I have always considered myself an integral part of making the movie and I never felt like I was a mere technician.

Looking back now, I was perhaps too eager to agree to do things, and I still am, nothing has changed there. If something is happening, I have always wanted to grab it. My colleagues at CBC were reluctant to try new things, they didn't want to shoot handheld for example, they'd rather have a camera on a tripod and they would not use small cameras to run around with; they were conditioned with the old British system, in a sense. A lot of times they would say no when they were asked to do things due to technical reasons, and they had difficulty being flexible with the conditions. On the other hand, the producers loved my eager attitude. I would adapt easily to the situation and would find a way within the circumstance to get what we needed. This compromised some technical aspects at times, but it made the producers feel very secure. My only system was to go get the magic happening, right now. If you had to wait for technical operations to be just right like steady cameras, back light, side light and these ratios and all that, the shots would be artificial. So I was very much into grabbing things.

At that time in the 1970s, CBC was a protagonist in developing Canadian culture and together with the National Film Board in Montreal they formed two amazing organizations that catered to the arts and promoted talent in this country. CBC was doing a number of movies each year so most Canadian actors, technicians, editors, and designers were trained by CBC and the NFB. Freelance camera people might do very few shows a year but I was so lucky to be on staff because I did ten to twelve shows a year as a CBC employee. Doing that number of shows gave me a lot of experience. The shows I talk about in this chapter are just a small sample.

Telescope *and* For the Record

In the early seventies, I was assigned to do a TV series called *Telescope* with Ken Kavanagh, filming nineteen episodes over two seasons. The premise was wonderful – famous people, mostly Canadians, doing interesting things all over the world. This included people like Gordon Lightfoot, actors John Vernon and Donald Sutherland, Farley Mowat, David Suzuki, Gerald Durrell, Arthur Erickson, Janis Ian, and many others. It was a half an hour show and was a mix of interviews and visuals. It involved a lot of travel with Canadians doing interesting things. One of the shows I did was with well-known and colourful journalist Ma Murray of Lillooet, British Columbia. On the train from North Vancouver through Horseshoe Bay to Lillooet, we passed

A Telescope *episode featuring the celebrity French-Canadian chef Madame Jehane Benoît.*

by the magnificent Howe Sound during sunset. Looking at the amazing vista for the first time, I said to Ma Murray, "if there's a heaven on Earth, there it is. There it is!" Ma turned to look at me, "Wait until you see Lillooet."

For *Telescope*, we had in-depth on-camera interviews alongside the visual aspect of the work of these characters. I was often doing the visual aspects spontaneously, without being too concerned with the technicalities. Consequently, the footage we got often had a gutsy feel to it. It had a sense of honesty and realism. Normally those things would be missed because most camera guys would say they needed time to set it up, well I didn't care. My casual, maverick take on things helped me a lot.

In 1972 Ralph Thomas and Stephen Patrick, the two current affairs producers at CBC, had the concept for a series called *For the Record* where a 90-minute dramatization with actors and a

In action through the cab window with John Vernon and his family, For the Record *in 1972.*

script would be set up against real events, thereby giving a feel of realism and bringing great production value to the scene. They were given the green light for this docudrama idea that set up socially relevant Canadian topics against the reality of the real event; what they called 'direct cinema'. Ralph requested that I be assigned to do the series as a DP.

I had shot some documentaries with Ralph prior to *For the Record* so we had a good working relationship. However, I had never shot dramas or fiction, so I thought it would be lovely, but my film department would not allow me to go ahead. They thought shooting drama took skills in lighting and understanding film chemistry that I did not have and offered names of others who they thought would be more qualified. But Ralph insisted on using me because he wanted a documentary style of filmmaker rather than what he called the "cardboard studio shooting." So my department had no choice and I did the first two seasons of *For the Record* for CBC. This was the start of my journey into doing fiction films.

The producers brought a whole who's who of known directors in Canada to elevate the series, especially the Quebec directors. Quebec has made some wonderful films in my mind in this country. They have a very strong identity, they have their own voice, they're not afraid, they're unique, they have flair, and their films have always interested me. I worked as Director of Photography (DP) with Claude Jutra, , who was doing some major work in Quebec such as *Mon Oncle Antoine*; Gilles Carle who did *The Plouffe Family*; and I remember working with Michel Tremblay who was doing a lot of stage work in Quebec like *Les Belles-Sœurs*, and *Hosanna*. Other directors who worked with us on *For the Record* were Don Brittain, who came from the Film Board and directed the first-ever IMAX film, and Peter Pearson, who was head of Telefilm Canada at one time.

Unfortunately what happened with *For the Record* was they started out with the premise of taking a dramatic script and setting it against a real event so they could use the ambiance of the real event to enhance the drama. In the long run, though, it didn't end up being that way because although the stories still came from journalistic sources, the execution became just like any other drama. It was sad because the first day on set, I was just on my own with a basic documentary crew with me for lighting and sound, and perhaps an assistant. Well, in the meantime, the trucks start rolling in for the makeup and hair and costumes just like any other production with a forty-men crew and there I was, standing there with my four-man crew. Nevertheless, I shot the first season with just this small crew. The unexpected payoff for me was is that of those three shows, two were nominated for best cinematography and the one show called *The Insurance Man from Ingersoll* became a big hit for the series. Through sheer necessities and the fact that I didn't know any better, I embarked on the path of using a minimal system, as opposed to the Hollywood system. *For the Record* was absolutely brilliant for me for getting my food in the door for doing fiction.

CBC Still Photo Collection

Catherine O'Hara, who was in the cast of a CBC pilot
Rimshots (*aka* Custard Pie) *with Dave Thomas and Andrea Martin.*

The Rimshots Pilot (1976)

Sometime around the time of *For the Record* I shot a pilot show for an ensemble of Second City improvisers including Dave Thomas, Andrea Martin, Saul Rubinek, Catherine O'Hara, and George Bloomfield directed it. It was great fun to work with these guys and I felt they were very talented, creative and full of fun. Often I couldn't even roll the camera because I would be laughing so hard. Dave would grab me by the shoulders and put my head behind the camera and say, "Vic, this is the eyepiece, this is where you put your eye, and I'll go in front and you can look at me now, okay?" There were scripts, but most of the time they would go off script and improvise. I think at the end the pilot worked very well but CBC didn't pick it up. It wasn't green-lit because the ensemble wanted control over the script but CBC was feeling nervous under those circumstances. The group of them formed *SCTV* with a few others, they went to Edmonton, and the rest is history. Readers might be amused to know

Martin LaVut the director and performers of War Brides, *along with performers including Wendy Crewson and Elizabeth Richardson.*

that George Bloomfield and I shot the famous *SCTV* opening sequence of televisions being thrown out onto the street from a tall building. Jim Carrey used to run around CBC too making his funny faces and all, but even though CBC was the feeding ground for a lot of great drama, it didn't quite connect with comedy talent at that time.

War Brides (1979)

CBC was the only major Canadian broadcaster doing period films and *War Brides* came along, which was about British women who met Canadian soldiers during the WWII. Martin LaVut, who used to be a stand-up comedian, directed it. He was a wonderful man who kept a really happy atmosphere on the set, against the very heavy subject matter. He allowed me to contribute a lot of creative input, which I loved. It was a big challenge for me because many of the characters' dreams and expectations took place on a travelling train. We didn't have the money or the technical equipment to shoot on a real train so the designer built a set in the studio and it became my joyful challenge to give the train the appearance of movement.

To give the feel of a moving train, we put the train on huge rubber inner tubes and had the boys rock it back and forth to give it a sense of movement I came up with the concept that when a train moves, light shifts from the outside shadows, whether it be from trees or tunnels. So once the lights were set and actors were in place on the train benches, my crew of half a dozen stage hands or so would run along outside the train with big heavy branches, then loop back and run along again to simulate the train moving through the shadows and light. We used various colour filters on the lights to have a shift in colour of the light when the sun would be setting, and once we got the hang of pacing the shadows when the stage hands ran and when the sound effects got added, it was a fantastic way of creating the illusion of travelling.

Elizabeth Richardson, Sonja Smits, Sharry Flett, and Wendy Crewson played the war brides. I remember the camera liked these actresses a lot. As a DP, I always operated my own camera, so I was always the first person watching the movie through my eyepiece, before there were monitors on the set. Operating the camera is half the fun of being a cinematographer, as you see the film being made, and you are the first one to watch it. At times, the actresses would look outside the walls of the train with an expression of *Who am I, where have I been, and where am I going?* All these emotions were moving across their faces and I was inspired to put a camera outside the mock train carriage windows. In those days, CGI was expensive and cumbersome and we didn't have the budget so the challenge was to create a sense of the train travelling through the countryside in the nighttime. We put a slide projector outside of landscape images and we projected them onto the window in front of the actresses and it softly spilled onto their faces. It did not quite work for the night scene so we brought in a 16 mm film projector and projected landscape scenes shot at night and it brought

*Getting assistance from my favourite camera assistant,
Neville Ottey, on a "dolly shot" for* Riel.

us an excellent result. This was a great experience for me and I
enjoyed the amazing collaboration with Martin LaVut. We went
on to do more films together, including *Charlie Grant's War*.

Riel (1979)

The biggest thing that happened in the late seventies was when
John Trent, a freelance producer that CBC used to worship, was
asked to do a film about Louis Riel. *Riel* was the biggest show
that CBC had ever done in the seventies and it was a co-production between CBC and John Trent's own production company.
Riel was a three-hour period story and they brought in celebrated Canadian actors from all over the world like Christopher
Plummer, William Shatner, Neville Shute, and Barry Morse.

John Trent asked me if I would like to be Director of
Photography on *Riel*. I had never done anything of this scale but
he and I had done a TV movie previously titled *Crossbar* and he
liked what we were able to do together, with an easy approach

*The "over the horse's rear" technique in action
for moving camera shots on* Riel.

and a kind of natural look. Though some of my colleagues spoke disparagingly of John and his methods, I did not see that and got along with him very well. John was always trying to find the way to make things work. I enjoyed his passion and positive energy.

Riel was sixty days of shooting – a long shoot in those days when we used to shoot an hour show in fifteen days. We were supposed to shoot it in Saskatchewan but the budget wouldn't allow it so we ended up building sets at Kleinburg Studios, just outside Toronto. Bill Beeton, the production designer, designed some wonderful sets and gregarious George Bloomfield, who by then had finished several seasons of *SCTV*, was brought in to direct. Raymond Cloutier and Roger Blay came in from Montreal to play Louis Riel and Gabriel Dumont. Leslie Neilsen played Major Crozier, and Christopher Plummer got into his role as Prime Minister John A. Macdonald. The movie generated a lot of publicity because it was one of the biggest film productions CBC had attempted to do. So we were at the forefront, and the

Christopher Plummer as John A. MacDonald in Riel, *expressing his vision to build a railway.*

media paid attention.

As we got into production there was a scene where Plummer, as John A. Macdonald, had a model train. It was Macdonald's vision to build a railroad to unify Canada and connect us all. So the engine of the model train was set up right in front of the lens with Plummer in the background having his brandy. The script had him get up and walk over to the little model of the engine and the scene builds up to when he says, "This is my dream. We will build a railroad to bring Canada together." It was a pivotal and dramatic scene for the film, where Macdonald expresses his dream of uniting the country through a railroad.

As the scene played out, Plummer put the brandy down, and moved toward the model of the engine, which was placed on a table in the foreground. He did his lines and we cut. George would usually turn to me at the end of the take to ask me if we needed another take. This time, I said to him, "I think we should do one more." He asked me if it was something technical. I replied, "Not really." Well, Plummer heard that and he just hit the roof, swearing, insisting that he knew exactly what the scene was about. I replied, "Mr. Plummer, I am just the camera man..." but he carried on into his rampage directed towards me. Plummer was an idolized actor at the time, and had just come off *The Sound of Music* so George, being the peacemaker, suggested we move on to the next scene.

In the evenings, John used to take Plummer to the Sutton Place Hotel in downtown Toronto and bring him to the set in the morning. Plummer got the star treatment, of course, and John and Christopher loved talking, both men being very gregarious. The next morning, John came running up to me and said, "I want to talk to you, I have a bone to pick with you." When I asked him what he meant he said, "What did you do to Plummer, he was so upset last night when I took him home." I stumbled through some kind of explanation and apology but later that morning back on set, George said, "Remember the scene we finished yesterday? I think we need another angle to finish it, so let's do another set-up from a different angle." What happened this time around on a fresh take was that Plummer, who was drinking brandy in the scene, played less drunk. As a result, his performance had much more impact as a powerful, and sober scene, telling the story of the foundation of this country. I think what happened was that Christopher was wondering why the camera guy would say 'one more take' when it wasn't a technical issue. After leaving the set, and I am speculating here, Plummer thought about my reaction and maybe decided that he was playing too drunk when he was giving his vision of uniting the country. At any rate, his performance was more calm and collected when give his empowering speech.

I, being young, intimidated, and not having quite the right vocabulary to respond to Christopher at the time, was tongue-tied and I couldn't explain myself to him. However, I've always admired him and felt he was brilliant as an actor. A few years later, I worked with Christopher again and I mentioned our experience on *Riel*. He just smiled.

One thing I have noticed in my career is every person

in front of the camera wants to do his or her best. Let's face it, who doesn't – we all do, whether we are Prince Charles or Christopher Plummer, or even myself – I like to look good on camera too. I feel that most people whoever they are or whatever status they have, want to be presented in the best light. That's basic human nature. After all, we're all the same – our needs, wants and our dreams. I've always worked with that human side of us as a camera man. So if you can strip people down so they do not feel threatened by you, you can connect with them on a human level. Even more important is that they think you are really curious about what they think. These elements boil down to honesty, sincerity, and curiosity.

My father often said "Don't ever be intimidated by anybody. Just remember no matter who they are, they are no different than us. They eat. They sleep. Our needs are all the same." We often get carried away with people's statuses. You are just like me, I am just like you. We play by different rules but at the end of the day, nothing is different. So I work on the human level and am not afraid of protocols because we are people. So when I when I work with eminent people, I am not nervous because I never get star-struck. I felt totally at home around Christopher Plummer as I do around tribal people in Kenya.

You've Come a Long Way Katie (1980)
My first film as a director for CBC was *You've Come a Long Way Katie* in 1980, which was a three-part miniseries, starring Lally Cadeau who played a popular television host addicted to alcohol and Valium. I filmed as well as directed the film. At the time I did *Katie*, I had very little experience directing, however, taking care of the technical aspects of directing was second nature to me by then. It was a little unusual that the director was always looking through the eyepiece of the camera the whole time as I did but as a result, I didn't get in the way of the lead actress, Lally Cadeau. Instead, she took the part and got fully immersed in it. She was in almost every scene and through the course of the film, she *became* alcoholic, she *became* distraught, and she totally became what Katie was. I learned that if an actor has a

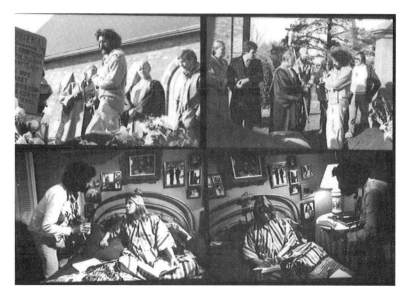

*Working with actors on the set of
You've Come a Long Way Katie (1980).*

meaty part, all a director has to do is to guide and let them be who they are because they, as the characters of the story, have a far stronger instinct of what and how to give the best performance. For the success of the *You've Come a Long Way Katie*, I give full marks to Lally; it has nothing to do with me, although I did two jobs on the series. Due to my lack of directorial experience, I did not get in her way and I learned a valuable lesson from it about performers and performance.

On the first day of shooting for *Katie*, the actors and crew, along with myself, showed up at the assigned townhouse location on a street of nearly identical row houses in Toronto. The house was meant to be dressed and all ready for us when we got there, but when we arrived, the home still had the old furniture. After a few distressed phone calls, we discovered that a house about three or four houses down was the one that was dressed. The set decorators had announced themselves to the owners of the home as being from CBC, had removed all their furniture, and replaced it with furniture that the designers had

Discussing the scene with Lally Cadeau and Booth Savage, along with Alan Harmon on You've Come a Long Way Katie.

chosen for the film. It was a strange but humourous start to the shoot. Thinking back at it, I chalk up the fact that the homeowners went along with all the random redecoration not because they thought they were getting something for nothing, but rather because they were nice, polite, and decent Canadians who didn't want to ruffle feathers.

When the reviews for *Katie* came in, headlines read "If you want to watch brilliance, turn to CBC tonight." There was a built-up of audience over the three consecutive nights it aired. Jeannine Locke, who wrote and produced the series, was an outsider to fiction, somewhat like me. We both got a lot of positive recognition for our work which was fantastic. Back then, the senior hierarchy like the executive producers, vice presidents, and heads of the departments were strictly policy makers and not filmmakers. Producers were the driving force. When a producer at CBC had an idea to present, it was very likely it would be green-lit. So the producer was totally in charge – there was no problem with distribution because it was going to go on television, there was no problem with money because the budget was already allocated, so the atmosphere was purely creative. For me, as a director or DP, I had an in-house crew, studio, equipment, and all the necessities. The challenge was entirely how to make something interesting with those resources and little money. The projects were led by the producer and the director and the pressure was purely creative. We didn't have to worry about the major problems in the industry today, such as the hierarchy, where the money is coming from, and the distribution.

In those days when our films were aired, we'd often have a party at home to celebrate. When the last episode of *Katie* aired, soon after, as usual, the phone calls started coming in from friends and family congratulating me. A phone call came in from Thunder Bay, Ontario from a woman who asked me if I had made this film. I said yes. There was a moment of silence and then she said, "I hate you." I told her I was very sorry to hear that but wanted to know why. She asked me, "Why did Katie have to die at the end?" I explained to her that the reason we dramatized this film is because a lot of women use alcohol to excess and when they combined the alcohol with Valium, it had a lethal effect. I told her we wanted to bring the subject out in the open. Then I heard crying over the phone and I said, "I am so sorry to upset you." She said, "I just wanted Katie to live because my own daughter died that way." I took in her grief for a moment and said, "You understand why we did this film then." She said, "I just wanted Katie to live because I just wanted some hope." By then I was crying and she was crying but when I receive emotional feedback like this, even though it may be bitter but sweet, my work becomes even more worthwhile.

PART II

Outside

Chapter 5

Filmmaking on the Outside

A FTER DOING *You've Come a Long Way Katie* in 1980, I got a number of offers to work outside the CBC. Various agencies and agents in Canada and Los Angeles offered to represent me as a director and although I was tempted, I had a strong loyalty for 'the corporation', which is what we called CBC, and was a bit insecure about leaving the fold. Jeannine Locke who had produced Katie, said to me, "You can't leave CBC, we're your family." I also felt I was with my family. And I thought, *Yeah you're right*, so I didn't leave.

I was very fortunate in that I was allowed to take on work outside the CBC, provided I had nothing scheduled at the time. Another part of the deal was that I would not get paid for my time away. The reasoning was simple; whatever I learned from the outside, I offered to bring back to the corporation. For example, at CBC we shot all our television shows in 16 mm and theatrical features were all 35 mm those days. My CBC colleagues were content that the experience I acquired outside with equipment and techniques would benefit my work inside the corporation.

The Naked Peacock (1975)

I must admit, there was a commercial film I did while working at CBC back in 1975 that was a bit crazy but a lot of fun. Dennis Hargreaves was a CBC producer who I'd worked with as an assistant cameraman on his series called *Children of the World*, which was a UNICEF and CBC co-production. Dennis

Wading out into the river on a shoot for
Children of the World, *with Dennis Hargreaves. 1971.*

was a passionate character and man of great integrity. It was for
Dennis that I did my first trip around the world for the series,
which was about the children of the world and their dreams and
aspirations. So I got to know Dennis pretty well.

Dennis asked me to work on a commercial film, *The Naked
Peacock*, which was the brainchild of a couple of Toronto lawyers. It was about nudism, to be shot across North America, particularly in California. At the time I was a little hesitant due to
the nature of the film. Nevertheless, at the same time, the subject was tempting.

Our initial plan was to visit the nudist colonies and talk to
people and film them doing their day to day tasks and such.
Then Dennis became concerned that it might be difficult to
get people at the camps to be in front of the camera so we hit
on the idea of hiring trained actors to 'play' nude instead of
relying on the actual nudists. We had a casting call at a Sunset
Boulevard hotel in Los Angeles for people who wouldn't mind

On location 1975 at the nudist camp for Naked Peacock.
In am in the back row, clothed.

being naked. Well, people were lined up all the way from the room on the second-floor of the hotel, down to the lobby, and out the front door, hoping for a chance to join our production. Only in California – if they get naked, who cares? It's an acting job. The interesting thing was that our Canadians, Dennis and the lawyer producers, were so shy when they were casting the show that they hardly looked up from their clipboards. They looked like they were ready to die with embarrassment when girls in line popped their tops open and the guys got ready to drop their drawers. I remember one guy saying, "Listen, I've got a great body, hey look at my ass, man," and girls saying, "I've got great tits, man, check it out," and the like. I wish I'd had a camera on Dennis and the producers that day.

But we ended up not using the actors. The members of the nudist clubs were actually more than eager to be part of the film, which made our lives very easy and a lot of fun. There was one scene where the members were to jump naked by parachute into their club out of a small plane. So, I took off with them to film this sequence. At a certain altitude, the jumpers would wait by the open door for the green light that meant 'jump'. Because of the strong incoming wind, the penis of the jumper by the door started rotating around just like a propeller. I found it funny, so I started filming a close-up of the rotating penis and then went up to his face. I did this shot for fun, so the editing boys would have a good laugh. To my surprise, when the film opened theatrically, that was the opening shot of the film. The camera starts on the propelling penis, and the voice says, "Let me introduce myself." Then the camera moves up to his face.

There was one nudist club we visited that would not allow us to keep our clothes on while we shot. I was pretty much okay with that, except I noticed that when I could, I would rest my camera in front of me; just a natural reaction to cover myself up – the same way Peter Sellers would hold his guitar in front of his private parts in *A Shot in the Dark*.

The film opened in Toronto at the Coronet Theatre right on Gerrard and Yonge Street, close to the CBC building, and there was a funny blurb in *The Toronto Star* about how the two CBC guys took time off to do this interesting film. The film had a good run at the box office.

Heartaches (1981)

In the seventies and eighties, any money that was spent on a feature film was allowed for tax credit. So 'outside', business was starting to take off. We were totally in love with Hollywood in those days and so if a name actor came to Toronto, the whole town would buzz, *Oh my God, Robert Redford is in town*, or *Elizabeth Taylor and Richard Burton are in town* – we were so completely enamoured by these stars. The era that started in the seventies and built up in the eighties involved big name American stars in dramatic films that were being shot in Canada. Since this was being done 'outside', the CBC was starting to take the back seat for the first time. We were no longer the only game in town, so to speak. The result was that the feature film industry in Canada started to come to life.

With Margot Kidder and Annie Potts on the
set of Heartaches.

In 1981 I shot my first 35 mm feature. The film was called *Heartaches* with Margot Kidder and Annie Potts, and directed by Don Shebib, who had done *Goin' Down the Road*. In *Heartaches*, a young wife, played by Annie Potts becomes pregnant, but her husband is not the child's father. She is afraid to tell him, leaves home on a bus, and meets a free-spirited woman, played by Margot Kidder. I loved working on it and this film further established my exposure to the outside world.

Margot Kidder was a hot star because of her Lois Lane role in *Superman*, so she generated a fair amount of Hollywood buzz, even though she was Canadian. She lived a pretty strong life and loved partying and drinking. By the time we started *Heartaches*, she knew that I could make her look her best for the camera, even if she had tied one on the night before. She had a great sense of humour and we got along great, especially since she knew I would do what I could to reduce her day-after-the-night-before appearance.

The slate says Heartburn *but this shot is the director,*
languishing on the set of Heartaches.

It was a summer film that we were shooting in November
and it was brutal. I remember the actresses, Margot and Annie
Potts, doing their scenes in summer dresses and breaking into
tears at the end, they were so cold. The whole film was shot in
very overcast conditions, mostly taking place at a picnic along
Toronto's Scarborough Bluff.

At the end of the film, there was scene that called for Margot
to slip and slide down a steep hill. Being a busy actress, she was
booked to leave for LA the next day, but a big problem came on
the day we were to shoot that scene; the sun decided to shine
and we had a beautiful blue sky to contend with.

In film days, as opposed to what we can do now with digital, there was not much we could do to match the sky. We were
shooting from a low angle and the blue sky was the dominant
feature in the frame, looming over Margot who was looking
down the bluff in her crisis moment of *should I jump or not.'*

I showed up on the set and for some reason I could not find

On location near High River, Alberta in 1982
for Jeannine Locke's Chautauqua Girl.

the director or any of the producers. The assistant director (AD) was there for a few minutes though, and before he left, he said it was impossible to shoot because the skies would never cut together. But since Margot was there, in costume and ready to do the scene, I made a call to go ahead, even though there was nobody else around. My thinking was that Margot had to leave for Hollywood the next day, every day of delay cost the production $100,000 and we had no other choice.

Somehow or other, it ended up that just Margot, my assistant camera man and I were left to do the scene and we all had the kind of personalities that said, "Let's just do it!" I took the camera on my shoulder, she tumbled down the hill, my assistant pulled focus and that was it. When we were all finished, people started drifting back onto the set reiterating their thoughts that we couldn't shoot the scene because it wouldn't cut together and we were able to say, "It's already done."

As an aside to the story, there was never a mention from

audience or critics that anything was wrong with the scene and I was complimented for the cinematography.

The lesson I learned was not to get bogged down with little things that don't make a difference to the story. Nobody but continuity geek fans will notice that the sky does not match perfectly or there was a sandbag left in the middle of the field where the actor's mark was meant to be taped. Actor shows up with a black eye? Shoot around it! The audience mainly concentrates on the story so better to get the scene shot than have the entire production fall apart.

Chautauqua Girl 1982

Jeannine Locke, who I had worked with on *The Family Prince. The Other Kingdom,* and *You've Come a Long Way Katie,* wrote and produced a TV movie called *Chautauqua Girl.* She had always wanted to write something about the travelling Chautauqua that was an ensemble of actors and musicians who would entertain in prairie towns in the 1920s. Jeannine had an extraordinary pulse for this county and knew Canada inside out historically. She loved to talk about how before the days of radio, the Chautauqua travelling tent show was the only way that rural Canadians could capture a glimpse of the larger world.

The location we found for the film near the town of High River, Alberta was greatly appealing to me. The prairies, starting from Manitoba and on into Alberta is the best canvas I've ever seen in my life for the camera. When I see something through the eyepiece of the camera that excites me, it brings all the energy in the world – it is quite different than what I experience with my naked eye. Jeannine brought in choreographer Rob Iscove to direct the show and Rob created delightful dance scenes in the show. I was hired as Director of Photography (DP).

One of my contributions generally as a DP is good preparation so the crew can stay ahead of the game. With a large crew, it is crucial to plan things out such as where the generator will go and where the cables will run. I do not do in-depth planning as to where the camera or the lights go, for example. To me, the joy of film is observing and discovering on the day, allowing the actors and the director to have the freedom to act on their instincts about the story and characters rather than worrying about limitations based on the camera. I enjoy going in cold and seeking what will be exciting in the moment – one can never fully plan for all the elements that come together on the day. Over the years, I've seen many directors come in with a plan, a shot list and a storyboard, but it seldom works out the way they've envisioned. I've learned to seek the best possible solutions instead of working against the flow. Actors and directors change their minds, and plans change due to uncontrollable forces such as the weather and shifting natural light – the main factor being nature itself, which you cannot control. I have learned to adapt myself, work with what I have, and discover a beautiful gem from the moment at hand.

The setting for our major location was a big tent, which worked very well for both interiors and exteriors. It was very well designed with a great use of colour. I wanted to shoot the exteriors during 'magic hour' light, which is a clear golden light in the early evening. However, to shoot that, it takes a lot of work to wrangle the animals, buggies and extras within that narrow window of time. Not only that, but as the light shifted, the grip guys would have to pick up the camera and dolly, the AD would have to clear the set and eyeline, and by then, we would have lost the light.

That is when I was able to put my news and documentary skills into action. If I saw something, I'd grab the camera say to the director or the assistant director, "Grab those two buggies right now, just get those damn buggies!" If the sun was moving a little bit, it wouldn't matter because I would be hand-holding the camera so it would be mobile and able to accommodate the changing light in seconds. The matter remains that you don't want hand-held shots for a period film, so to steady the shot, I'd get my assistant to stand behind me. I'd lean against him and tell him, "Don't breathe." We didn't have millions of Hollywood dollars to spend on our productions so I used my own *"gung-ho* get the shot" technique.

Chautauqua Girl was screened at various places, including

With Anne Wheeler in Alberta.
Working with Anne and her talented actors was always enjoyable.

one event at Rideau Hall, which was attended by Prime Minister Pierre Trudeau, CBC president Pierre Juno, and other dignitaries. I remember Mr. Juno commenting on the cinematography and how wonderful it was. My answer was, "Sir, it doesn't have much to do with me. It's the country and how beautiful it is. You have just to point the camera. I wish we were using our backyard more instead of doing more urban films." *Chautauqua Girl* did well for Jeannine, for director Rob Iscove, and for the two lead actors, Janet-Laine Greene and Terence Kelly who were wonderful to work with.

Loyalties (1987)

In mid-eighties, Anne Wheeler directed her first feature, *Loyalties*. I did not know Anne but I got a call from her asking me if I'd be interested in working on the film as a DP. When I heard that the film was going to be shot in Alberta, I jumped at it. It was a well-written script by Sharon Riis, featuring Susan

Wooldridge, Kenneth Welsh, Tantoo Cardinal, and Tom Jackson.

Anne and I hit it off pretty well. I found her very funny. She has a great sense of humour and is very easy-going, yet very focused. The screenplay called for Lac La Biche, Alberta. Because of her documentary background and attention to historical detail, Anne felt that it was the right place to shoot. I questioned her decision because once you bring in the camera, you're changing it anyway so why feel guilty about changing the location? I was disappointed in the location and felt the canvas was not as beautiful as it could be. Lac La Biche, to me, wasn't the prairies that I was in love with, though it served the story as needed. Anne acknowledged that and said to me, "The next time we work together, I'm going to give you a location where you want to shoot." Overall we had a lot of fun doing the film together and I loved the experience of working with the actors.

There was a scene in the movie where the two women go into the water and they struggle, with one of them nearly drowning and the other saving her. When we saw the scene, I said to Anne, "It would be nice to go underwater with the camera and watch the struggle from underwater." She thought it was a good idea so we talked to the producer and he agreed to the expense, but we had to bring the camera, its mount and housing, plus an operator and his team all the way in from Florida. We talked about the budget and if we could afford it for the two or three shots we needed. In the end we decided to do it.

On the day we came to shoot the scene, Susan and Tantoo went into the lake along with the camera operator and the guy came up out of the water saying, "There's no visibility in there, we can't see a thing." As it turned out, it was the time of year when algae floats in the lake and beyond a foot away, it was pitch black under the water. Anne with her great sense of humour just laughed and we realized that if we had asked any local, they could have told us that at this time of year the algae takes over the lake. We spent all the money, didn't get the shots, but the film worked very well anyway. As the cinematographer on a film, I worry about small things that get away but most often the film works like a charm anyway. The lesson I learned was to think deeper before I open my big mouth.

The actors delivered very powerful performances. At the climax of the film, there is a scene where Ken's character chases a young girl to molest her. It was a rainy night and a big set-up for the camera. Knowing the intensity of the scene, everything had to be prepared so the actors could do the scene as quickly as possible. Looking through the lens and watching Ken perform this scene was very eerie. He was completely in character, but as soon as Anne called 'cut', I watched Ken walk away from it all instantly. It was a difficult scene for Ken and I saw for the first time how a great actor rises to the occasion, despite all the difficulties. I was moved by Ken's abilities as an actor.

Bye Bye Blues (1989)

The next film I did with Anne was *Bye Bye Blues*, which remains to this day a truly iconic Canadian film on many levels. Anne was true to her word that she had made to me from *Loyalties* days, about locations. She said to me, "Okay Vic, now you tell us where you want to shoot." Besides being able to go back to India where the film starts, we travelled around Alberta and found some great locations out by High River and Drumheller.

Earlier, I had worked with the actress Rebecca Jenkins as a director/DP on a CBC comedy film called *Family Reunion*. I thought Rebecca was right for the part, with her naturally lovable personality. Also, I knew she had a good voice. Anne subsequently cast her as the lead. *Bye Bye Blues* is a period film set during World War II about a woman to comes home to Alberta after living in India with her military husband who does not come back for years. It was a personal story for Anne because it was actually based on her father who was in the army stationed in India and was then sent to Singapore. Anne's mother, a talented pianist and singer, came back home to Alberta and waited for her husband to return from the war.

In *Bye Bye Blues*, I came much closer to photographing the beauty of Alberta and at the same time we were faithful to the story. We spent weeks out there and loved it. The combination

*Rebecca Jenkins saying hello to an elephant
on the Indian set of Bye Bye Blues.*

of music in the show, Anne's humour, Rebecca Jenkins' warmth, plus shooting in Alberta made it a wonderful experience.

The opening of the film starts in India, and it was interesting to witness the practical-mindedness of the Indian crew. I find that the way things are set up in North America, and especially in Hollywood, is quite often in the way of making a good film. The reason is because rules and regulations of the unions and different departments dictate the way things should be done. It's great, except small productions cannot always afford to fully comply. By the time small productions go that route, you can lose the honesty of the piece by losing the spontaneous essence of the content. That said, there are times, within reason, that one can bypass the rules, if they are unnecessary.

The purpose of putting a light in a certain place is to enhance the naturalness of the scene in whatever way the cinematographer wants. The scene I am thinking of from *Bye Bye Blues* is when we were shooting in India and Daisy, played by Rebecca, goes to an army base to find her husband. I remember telling the gaffer Suzanne, who was my lady friend at the time too, to remind the Indian gaffer to place an HMI light on a high stand that I had requested earlier. The light was supposed to be fairly high up, and meant to give a soft fill light across the acting area. Suzanne said "Vic, they told me they were going to have it, just calm down." A high stand is a piece of equipment that is very commonly used in the industry.

The day came to shoot the scene, so I said to the guy, "Rahim,'" Rahim was his name, "Where is the stand?" Rahim said, "It's here sir, don't worry, where do you want the light?" I told him, "I want the light about twenty feet up there." He repeated, "Yes, yes, sir, no problems. When do you want it?"

"Right now!" I said. Rahim clapped his hands and four guys came in with pads on their shoulders and they formed a pyramid by sitting on each other's shoulders, holding the heavy light up to the height of twenty feet, steady as a rock. Well, everyone on the set broke out laughing and instead of concentrating on the scene they were watching this circus. But we did the scene and the shot is in the film. That's India for you. In many places like India, Vietnam, Cambodia, and China, they make things work out somehow. It's worth learning from.

I have another example of that – a sunrise scene on another film I did a few years later in India called *The Burning Season*, which featured a talented Indian actor Om Puri and was directed by Harvey Crossland. I insisted to the tech crew that the equipment would have to be ready the moment the sun peeked over the horizon and that would mean they would have to be there to set up in the middle of the night. They said "Yeah, that's life, no problem." There were camels in the scene in front of a prop temple and dozens of extras so it was a pretty big set up. I was going to go a couple of days before to check out the point on the horizon where the sun would come us so I could mark where the crane should go. Sadly, I got distracted and forgot to do that.

The night before we were meant to shoot that scene, I

pepped up the tech crew to get ready, but inside I was said to myself *Oh God I have no idea where the sun comes up.* There we were out there in the middle of the night, the camels, all the extras in their saris and our two actors, and I was petrified inside because I had no idea where to put the camera. I hadn't done my homework. The guys were saying, "Well, sir where would you like the crane to go?" I said, "Oh, just give me a few minutes." I was thinking, How can I get out of this trouble now?

From my experience setting up a crane takes a lot of time – in Canada it would take the crew an hour at least, then there is the balancing with the counterweights and other things. So I asked the guy "How long is it going to take you?" and he said "Five minutes." The five minutes was perfect for me because I knew that about ten minutes before the sun comes up, the sky gets a little lighter along the horizon.

Anyway, I started to see and feel a tiny hint of light emerging and at that moment I knew exactly where to put the camera and within five minutes they had the crane done. I sat in the front and they pulled me up – everything was done so quickly! First take! We only had one chance to get the shot because of the light and you'll see it used in the film. In the scene, sun is just coming up and you see a camel in front of the sun and the camera pulling back and there's a little temple and people are walking slowly. I could never have done that in Canada because the safety standards were so strong. I took a chance of course – falling eight feet – but I always took chances. That kind of practicality is especially valid when you don't have much money on a film, or if you are out in the middle of nowhere.

Similarly, Chinese crews were fast and practical in setting up things, and in a very precise manner. I write of my experiences on the 2002 TV series *Flatland* featuring Dennis Hopper in a subsequent chapter; a production where there was flashy ancient warrior-style high wire flying. If Canadian crews of the day could have seen how the Chinese were doing some of these daredevil things, they would have freaked out

– the Chinese crews worked so fast it made me dizzy. Things are changing for the better now on both sides. In Canada, small films have more leeway, and on the other side, in India and China, they have better technology, bigger budgets and better equipment. Therefore, the gap is closing on both sides.

Chapter 6

Challenges and Satisfactions

IN 1987, Ivan Fecan was brought in from NBC to become director of programming at CBC and he was very progressive. The official line was that they wanted the ratings to go back up and wanted more viewership, but I knew intuitively that the CBC was about to make a shift into thinking more commercially. Canadians were developing a taste for American network entertainment and CBC wanted to become more competitive. I saw the writing on the wall, so I figured it was time to make my move into even more freelance work. My mother died too in 1987 and that hit me pretty hard.

Luckily for me, I had done outside work like the films I had done with Anne Wheeler and it was not difficult to find jobs. I did the *Alfred Hitchcock Presents* series as a DP and as a director, and a documentary called *Falashas* at about the same time, which was about black Jews in Ethiopia. My foray into the freelance world created some jealousy from the freelancers because they felt I had the best of both worlds. They figured I had a pay slip coming from CBC but what they didn't realize is that I didn't get paid when I was not working there. But still, I must admit, I had the security. I paid a price for five or six years in the mid-80s when I did some of the best work of my career but my peers, who gave out awards and nominations, did not care to recognize me. How I know all this is that a few drunken phone calls came in and that's when the honesty kicks in, as in, "Goddammit, you're taking all the jobs away." My colleagues were not always kind

Working with Lindsay Wagner on episode of
Alfred Hitchcock Presents *called "Prism" in 1988.*

and I felt they should talk to the clients and chat up their own skills, not take it out on me.

Dancing in the Dark

Over the years I have had the privilege of working on films with large budgets but then there are films like *Dancing in the Dark*, which was done from start to finish on only about $600,000, as I recollect. I admire the whole cross-section of films. What I discovered is that the best work I did was often on the smaller films because the DP can take on a bigger role. Consequently, I was more a part of the film than on a larger budget film. It was the first film for Leon Marr who adapted the screenplay from a book by Joan Barfoot and he had a very clear vision of what the film should be about and how it should look.

Dancing in the Dark was all set in one house and was about

Martha Henry during her transformation from heavenly to hellish in Dancing in the Dark.

a woman who was happily married and whose house was her castle. As the film progresses, the castle becomes a prison when she discovers that her husband is not who she thinks he is. So the whole milieu changes as she loses control. The house was the main character in the film and so as a DP, I had to consider how the house was going to make its transition from heaven to hell. Martha Henry, a well-known Stratford actor, played the lead. It was a very visual film and her acting was highly physical, so the non-verbal action came through profoundly. It was very challenging for Martha and for us, figuring out how to sustain this piece, the internal work, for ninety minutes. Martha Henry was brilliant in conveying all the emotions without saying a word.

I felt strongly that for this film we needed the right kind of house to sustain interest on the big screen for ninety minutes, and Leon was completely supportive. Since we did not have much money, the transformation had to take place in the house as easily and cheaply as possible. For that to happen, we made a collective effort to get around the constraints. We found a perfect house in the Rosedale area of Toronto, but we didn't have much money to hire experienced designers, set decorators, props people, and grip guys, so reality set in quickly. I always say we should allow ourselves to think big first and then let practicality settle in, and my theory held fast in this case. We were able to bring in energetic young people who were just keen to do it, so I felt pretty good in one sense because I was able to experiment.

We designed every little thing in the film with the vision in mind of turning a palace into a prison. We worked with the colours and lighting, but mostly with the props. For example the flower vases, tablecloths, and cutlery subtly changed as the scenes progressed. We didn't set out to create a barren appearance because then it would have been a gimmick. I didn't want people to be conscious of the set changes; it was a subtle manipulation done in such a way that people would be drawn to concentrate on the actors and the story, but be affected subconsciously by the colours, light, and props. It worked well, the film went to Cannes, and Leon Marr became a director to be taken seriously.

Love and Hate: The Colin and JoAnn Thatcher Story

I remember the producer Bernard Zukerman came up to me one day at a watering hole on Bay Street, close to CBC where I was visiting some friends, and said, "I hear you left CBC, take a look at this script. See if you might be interested in shooting it." It was the Colin and JoAnn Thatcher story. Now, I didn't remember at the time who Colin Thatcher was, nor am I normally a very enthusiastic reader, but I ordered a drink, found a quiet corner of the bar and read the 180-page script in one sitting, something I had never done before. It was a perfectly compelling story about a Saskatchewan politician who was going through a nasty divorce and allegedly hired a hit crew to murder his wife. Suzette Couture wrote a powerful screenplay, which was titled *Love and Hate*. I told Bernie right away that I would love to do it.

For this show, we needed crystal clear air for the shoot,

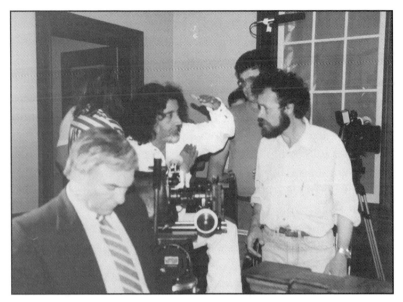

With Ken Welsh and the crew
on the set of Love and Hate: The Colin and JoAnn Thatcher Story.

With director Francis Mankiewicz on the set of
Love and Hate: The Colin and JoAnn Thatcher Story.

which we found in Saskatoon, where the crime had actually happened. This is nothing like the dusty air of India which is soft and smoke-filled, giving a romantic and painterly look. Instead, the clear air allowed me to push the sharp light into a sort of a hardness, which we needed for this very dark story.

A superb actress, Kate Nelligan, played JoAnn Thatcher and a talented actor, Ken Welsh, played Colin Thatcher. We shot in the winter in Saskatoon and one evening, Francis Mankiewicz, the director of the film and I staged a street scene based on photos of the actual crime, with specific types of ambulances, police cars, and many other exact details. We had a big crowd turn up and someone remarked that, "God, it looks just like the real time – *déjà vu*." Some bystanders were worried that there was a Colin Thatcher copycat murder or something; I guess it brought back memories for them.

We all did very well with the film on the award circuit. It was one of the highest-rated shows on CBC and it was also one of the few shows sold to the American networks. We all received many awards, validating the movie. I think Canadians are attracted to watching little slices of our more notorious past.

Cold Comfort (1987)

Peter Simpson, a producer I had worked with on the movie *Norman's Awesome Experience*, asked me to direct *Cold Comfort* because he thought I could bring a cinematic feel to the film. The story was based on a stage play by Jim Garrard and it is about a travelling salesman, played by Paul Gross, who becomes a prisoner in a big power struggle between a father and a daughter. Besides Paul Gross in the cast, Maury Chaykin played the dad, and Cindy Preston was to play the daughter.

Ray Sager was a producer who used to work at Norstar Film Entertainment alongside Peter Simpson and Ilana Frank. I had done a couple of films with them as a DP in the past, and Ilana Frank was very much into making a film based on a known Canadian stage play, *Cold Comfort*, by Jim Garrard. It was Ray Sager who brought me to the attention of Ilana to direct the film. This was my first feature film as a director.

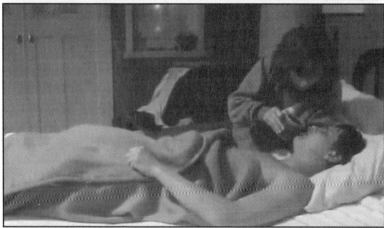

Cold Comfort *with Margaret Langrick, Paul Gross, Maury Chaykin.*

It was a difficult show to do because it was a winter film all based in a snowstorm but we shot it in the summer. One of the reasons I took the film is because it was set in Saskatchewan and was meant to be shot there. Well, it didn't happen that way; we ended up shooting it in the middle of the summer in Toronto.

The first day of the shoot went pretty well with Maury Chaykin and Cindy Preston but that night I got a call from the producer, Ilana Frank. She said, "If you are standing, you'd better sit down." She said that Cindy had been in a car accident. My first reaction was shock and I wanted to know, "How is she doing? Is she alright?" Ilana told me she was badly hurt, was going to be all right, but that we would have to recast because she was going to be unavailable for at least six months.

What a great start to my debut as a director! I felt it would take some time to replace Cindy for the film. However, for budget reasons, the producers wanted to stay on schedule. Ilana and Ray did a great last-minute casting job and were able to find Margaret Langrick, who had just done *My American Cousin*. Margaret came out from B.C. and jumped right into the role as Dolores. She was so right for the role, as if the part was written just for her. Margaret brought a fresh youthful innocence, but at the same time, added a bit of a bizarre quality to the character. She was brilliant and also very easy to work with. In a sense, I missed Cindy but I had a chance to work with Cindy Preston again years later on *Whale Music*, in fact Paul Gross, Maury Chaykin and Cindy Preston all came in on that project, as if it were a reunion.

There is a long and wonderful scene in *Cold Comfort* when Paul Gross' character is chained up as a captive by Maury Chaykin's character. My instructions to Maury were, "He's chained over here, sit, start the scene and make sure you give him enough distance so he doesn't catch you." He thought about it a bit and then said, "Can I have a little box of chocolates." The props man went and got him a box of chocolates and he played the scene eating chocolates. We did a master shot first, a wide shot, and I saw him eating chocolates now and then. During notes I said to Maury, "I'm not sure the chocolate idea is going

*Cold Comfort was set in a prairie winter landscape
but we actually shot in summer in Ontario.*

to work because we are going to do a lot of takes. I've got a lot of coverage to do." I was thinking that he was going to have to go through six or seven boxes of chocolates for continuity. Maury sighed and said, "Oh no Vic, it will be good for the scene" basically martyring himself for the artistic effect.

I remember hearing Paul snickering a bit because he knew Maury far better than I did, they were, in fact, close friends. We did the scenes and we did so many takes on it Maury must have gone through at least two or three boxes of chocolates. I felt sorry for him because for the sake of the art, poor guy had to go through all that. I told the story to Ilana Frank, who was Maury's ex-wife and she started to laugh. I said, "Don't you feel sorry for him?" She laughed and said, "That's just an old trick of Maury's. He just bloody well loves chocolate."

It was a very hard call when it came to committing to the ending of this film. This is a common problem because scripts are often written with a certain ending but during the making of the film, one senses it's simply not the right ending. Most the time, I find that the beginning and the middle work out but the ending is a bit problematic. So was the case with *Cold Comfort*. With *Cold Comfort*, we were playing around right to the last minute about the ending. Should Maury Chaykin's character die at the end or not? Should Margaret Langrick's character take off with Paul Gross's salesman character for a happily-ever-after future?

Maury and Paul made their voices heard and we gave the plot of the film a good hard look, discussing the changes that came with the chemistry between the actors. The film's signature enigmatic closing scene evolved as a result of the good hard look we took at the story curve. We didn't have to shoot any additional scenes to formulate the ending that we did, it was all a matter of choices made in the editing room.

I give full credit to Paul Gross and Maury Chaykin for their contributions to Cold Comfort, adding a lot more to it than was on the page. Paul Gross, besides being a younger Paul Newman both in looks and in acting talent, was a very good writer and thoughtful improviser. There's a scene where Margaret Langrick undresses at the beginning of the show. Basically she is inviting his attention and the scene is written that he does not respond. Paul was uncomfortable because he was sensitive and conflicted about his performance motivations. Instead of not responding, Paul turned his back and walked away to the window. I saw the opportunity, took that cue from Paul and placed her reflection in the window so he could still watch her reflection as she undressed; a tactic that explained the action and reaction, carrying the plot along. The combination of Paul's instinct and my follow-up made the scene more interesting. I felt this was a better placement for Paul to watch her and at the same time to dramatize the film.

Cold Comfort worked very well, despite all the problems of shooting a prairie film in Ontario, a winter film in the summer, losing the lead actress, and the six-month break before doing the opening and closing scenes where we needed the snow. That year (1987) at the Genie Awards there were three films at the top of the heap; Denys Arcand's *Decline of the American Empire*, *Bye Bye Blues* that I shot, and *Cold Comfort* that I directed and shot. *Bye Bye Blues* had eleven nominations. Although the cinematography was very much in the forefront of *Bye Bye Blues* and was one of the most talked-about aspects of the film, I was not nominated. *Cold Comfort* was a huge success with the audience, with five nominations. Even though the film did well, I directed and photographed it but I was not nominated in those categories. I've been on many juries since then and I know how it works. I felt the directors did not take me seriously as a director, meanwhile the cinematography judges felt I was no longer one of them. It could be that I got caught between that or could be anything else. But I know that many people were empathic towards me. Sid Eidelman, who had a column in *The Toronto Star*, was particularly kind to me. He picked both and me as 'Man of Year in the Entertainment Business' that year. That was very satisfying.

Chapter 7

Ripple Effects

ACH FILM I'VE DONE has taken me places I have never been before, with new locations and new knowledge. In the 1990s, the stories that I explored and the people I met, replete with the wild collection of back stories, show that if you go with the flow and pay attention, each film will pave the way to another idea or opportunity.

Millennium: Tribal Wisdom and the Modern World (1992)

I thought then, as I still think now, that the theme of 'tribal wisdom' and the modern world was, and still is, an amazing idea for a series, before all this wisdom disappears. Adrian Malone, who had produced and directed *The Ascent of Man* and *Cosmos* series for television was attracted to the concept for the same reason I was. Producers Michael Grant and Richard Meech had seen my film *Solitary Journey*, the theme of which revolved around a simple question: *What is there to conquer in your life, the external Everest or the internal Everest?* The simplicity of *Solitary Journey* resonated with the producers.

At the time, I had a unique choice; I had left CBC, was mostly freelancing, and my LA agent had a glamorous feature film offer for me. It was a difficult decision to go to Hollywood or take *Millennium*. I decided to take on the job of directing and shooting a ten-part documentary series shot around the world titled *Millennium* because I felt it was a chance of lifetime and it would be shame to pass up. After all, what makes my life rich is not money or the fame, but the experiences of life and *Millennium* was that opportunity. I knew the series would take me to places I would never go to again. Working with Adrian Malone was also a draw for me.

The first episode of the series I did for them was called 'Touching the Timeless' and was about the Huichol people, Indiginous people who live in the state of Jalisco in Mexico, and who take a annual pilgrimage into the desert to explore the spiritual world. I went with them to the desert for ten days where they took peyote. They were dancing and singing, supposedly finding peace of mind and become closer to their God. I don't take drugs but I observed what they did and accepted that it was a worthwhile experience, in keeping with their tribal traditions.

However, at the end of the pilgrimage, by tradition they sacrifice a cow. I asked them if they really needed to go through this because I was uneasy about it. They said that since I was uncomfortable and I needed to be there to film the scene, they would, instead, slaughter a goat. I do not remember arguing with them about it, but that night they tied the goat up outside my tent. All night long I could hear the baby goat bleating its heart out and I felt bad. I grew up as a vegetarian but after coming to Canada, I began to eat meat but I never liked being non-vegetarian. I could not sleep at all that night listening to sound of this goat so as morning came around, I cut the goat loose and she took off. When the Huichol people came around at sunrise and realized the goat was gone, the tribe practically went berserk. They thought it was a bad omen and that the gods were not happy so they brought in about eight or ten cattle to sacrifice instead and I had to shoot and witness the scene of this terrible slaughter. For the first time, I saw that the animals wanted to live as much I did. It was a bloodbath. That was the last time I ever ate beef.

Despite this unsettling experience, I went ahead and did episodes in Nepal and Kenya and that's when the two producers requested if they could do the tribal side of filming

*With my assistant John Davidson on location in
Mexico shooting Millennium.*

and I would take over the modern-world side. David Maybury-Lewis, the anthropologist who hosted the show, was brilliant and a real gentleman. On the modern side of the show, Adrian Malone decided to direct a portion of it himself and he wanted me to shoot it. We spent some time in Europe, doing just that, although with a bit of tension. I was disappointed because Adrian took the show in the direction of more analysis, intellectualizing every theme, as opposed to what I thought it was going to be: simple and honest as spoken by the tribal people. As opposed to dissecting, I thought the series would be us listening and observing these tribal people.

Overall, I think if *Millennium* had adhered to its original premise and maintained its theme, it would have been more effective. BBC in the UK, PBS in the States, and Global in Canada picked up the show anyway and we received many nominations and awards.

Out on the ice flow for Trial at Fortitude Bay, *with Lolita Davidovich. 1994.*

Trial at Fortitude Bay (1994) and the Americans

Chris Zimmer of Imagex in Halifax, loved *Cold Comfort* and in 1994 offered me the opportunity to direct a CBC TV movie called *Trial at Fortitude Bay*, set in Iqaluit on Baffin Island in Nunavut – back then it was Northwest Territories. It was about a young lawyer who defends an Inuit boy for a violent crime, only to find out that the Inuit have their own kind of justice system. Lolita Davidovich was cast to play the defence lawyer and Henry Czerny played the Crown prosecutor who was her adversary – wonderful actors, both of them.

At the last minute before we started shooting, Chris Zimmer was short $150,000 in the budget to make the film and the whole project was in jeopardy. A production company in Manitoba came to our rescue. They loved the script and brought in the money. The co-production went well until the end. When the shoot was over, our co-producer took over the post production and I made the mistake of not insisting on doing my director's

*More than once, I had to bundle up against the
elements shooting in Canada.*

cut of the film before I moved onto the next production.

Shortly after *Trial* was completed, I got a call from my agent
Ralph Zimmerman who told me that the producers from LA
were coming up to do a film in Toronto for Showtime Network.
He said they'd seen some of my work and they wanted me to
direct it. I hadn't done much work for the Americans up until
that time, just some *Spencer for Hire* DP work, so this would be
my first foray dealing one-on-one with an LA-based film company. I was very busy at the time so I wasn't at all pressured to
work for the down-south people; it didn't really matter to me,
but at the same time I was intrigued.

It was a family film, which I liked. However, my agent Ralph
said, "They would like to see your last film." So I asked Ralph to
show them *Trial at Fortitude Bay*. A couple of days later, Ralph
phoned me again saying, "I'm sorry Vic but they passed on you."
I responded "Oh, it's all right, happens all the time, it's part of the
game." After I had finishing expressing my nonchalance, I asked

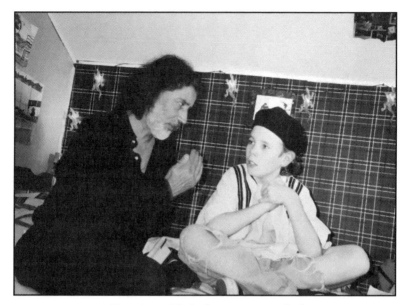

Chatting with the human Legend of
Gator Face *actor, John White. 1994.*

him, "Just do me one favour, Ralph. Find out what made them
pass on me. I might learn something about American thinking."

Ralph laughed and said, "They'll never call, you know that."
I said, "You can try, you never know." So anyway, he did request
a call and a few days later I got a call from the Head of the Family
Unit at Showtime and she said, "Hello Vic, this is Lori Kahn from
Showtime in New York and you had requested I call about why
we passed on you." I said "Thank you so much for calling. I was
just interested to know what you didn't like in the film you saw?"
There was a pause. Lori went on to say, "Well I liked the film and
the premise, but we didn't think the ending worked." I said, "You
are absolutely right," and I went on to explain the ending I had
shot and had not been implemented. She said, "That's brilliant;
why didn't you use it?" I explained that the producer who took
over concocted a different ending to the film, despite my objections. And I made a mistake that I did not do my director's cut
at the time.

I knew I didn't have the job and I was being myself so I said,

*Mr. T., who I worked on in
his series. We enjoyed each other's company.*

"Tell me Lori, when you do a film for the network, who controls the budget?" She said, "Well, we do." "Tell me Lori, who controls the final script?" "Well, we do that," she said. "Who controls the main lead actors?" "Well, we do" she said. "Who controls the final cut?" "We control it." After this last volley of questions, I paused to summon my courage and said, "Well what kind of nonsense is that? You take all the pillars of a director's work and if it doesn't work, then you blame the director? You're controlling it!" There was complete silence.

Well, a few days later they called me back. They wanted me to do the film. I ended up doing five films for Showtime after that, three of which were Emmy nominated: *In His Father's Shoes*, starring Lou Gossett; *Sea People* starring Hume Cronyn; and *The Legend of Gator Face*.

From my limited experience, I feel like it's not easy to get into the door of the film industry in the USA. There is a hesitation, however once you have earned their trust by giving them a well-received film, the relationship then becomes much more trusting. In Canada, I have found a somewhat different scenario. No matter how many films you have done in the past, you still have to go through the same steps over and over again. It's frustrating. It's equally frustrating because most of the films in Canada are funded through various funding agencies with their own mandate. Consequently, it becomes a film made by committees, and not necessarily in the best interest of the project. On the other hand, I come from the environment where one was given much more independence as a filmmaker.

Margaret's Museum (1995)

I had a chance to work with Chris Zimmer again in 1995 when he asked me to shoot *Margaret's Museum*. The script was based on Sheldon Currie's short story, a well-known Nova Scotia writer, and the script was developed from there. Mort Ransen, a very experienced National Film Board director, along with Gerald Wexler, adapted the screenplay from the short story. It was an excellent adaptation which attracted Helena Bonham Carter and others. Mort Ransen, who directed the film, was very kind to me and encouraged my cinematic input. We shot in Cape Breton, Nova Scotia, and in Scotland.

Helena Bonham Carter, who was cast as Margaret MacNeil, came into town straight from the airport after dropping her bags at the hotel and met with us at a bar for dinner. Straight away she wanted to know about the film and what the Cape Breton accents were like – she was right into it, even after flying all the way over the Atlantic. We were polite, asking her if she would like to have a little rest and such but she was ready to get underway.

Helena and I connected well and used to talk quite a bit. The tremendous part was that here was a young woman who was an A-list actor – she had already done a lot of important work like *A Room with a View* and *Howard's End* – who wanted to get straight to work, unlike most of the Hollywood stars who would be more interested in the comforts of their environment rather than working on the film. Instead, Helena was right in the trenches with us, totally engaged every day with what we

Scenes from Margaret's Museum, *with Kate Nelligan as Catherine MacNeil and Helena Bonham Carter as Margaret MacNeil.*

had to do to get things done with minimum fuss.

There was a scene in *Margaret's Museum* where Margaret had her first-ever shower; as the story went, she'd never had a shower before in her life because showers didn't exist in homes in those days. She finds out that there is a shower at the coal mine so she wants to try it out. The scene called for nakedness so she just disrobed and took a shower. Those scenes are often difficult to shoot due to the nature of them. Often we have closed sets and nudity was camouflaged or choreographed carefully because of the air of tension. It was refreshing how easy it was with Helena. Helena was comfortable playing the scene naked; for her it was no big deal at all. Her attitude freed our work behind the camera because we were fully at ease to do our work. Otherwise, it can be really awkward, as it had been in *Loyalties* where the actress doing a love scene insisted upon being completely covered in clothing.

It was great to see this professionalism on the part of Helena who read the script, understood, and accepted it. Her performance overall was full of confidence and spirit which made for a joyous experience for everyone.

I have found this commitment and professionalism with many English actors. Perhaps, it's because most of them come from a theatre background and training as opposed to the Hollywood actors. I found from my little experience that most English actors are actors first, and then they are stars. In Hollywood, they are often stars first, and then they are actors, but there are always exceptions. At least, this is what I have felt with my experiences.

The Hidden Dimension (1996)

Sally Dundas, a known Toronto producer, called me one day, saying they needed some pickup shots for *Gorillas in the Mist* and asked me if would I could fly to Germany to take it on. I was intrigued because it was an IMAX shoot and I had never shot IMAX before so I jumped at the opportunity, especially given that the production would nicely round out my skills

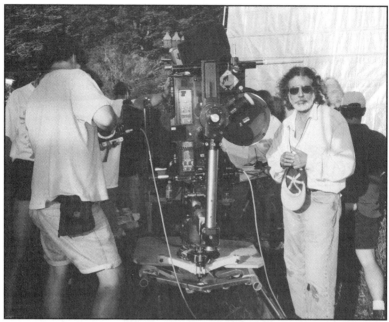

Working on The Hidden Dimension. *Here you see the full splendour of the IMAX camera.*

with just about every type of film camera.

A few years later, I got another call from the same producer asking me if I would be interested in working with Paul Cox, an Australian who I knew from his directorial work on a film I loved called *Man of Flowers*. The film this time, which Paul was to direct, was called *The Hidden Dimension* and was not only IMAX but also 3D. I told them I had no experience shooting in 3D, but they were happy to have me anyway because they had assigned me a camera operator, Noel Archambault, who knew the IMAX system inside out and had worked on a number of other IMAX films. The main shooting location was just outside Saint John, New Brunswick and working the camera was a serious learning curve for me. It was the first fully dramatic film shot for IMAX, so I suspect a lot of the crew members were feeling the same pressure.

When I tried to follow my instincts and set up shots as I normally would, Noel might say, for instance, that my lens choice and the camera movement were not the right way to go in the 3D world with the huge IMAX cameras. I wanted to push the boundaries and the restrictions of 3D, whereas Noel wanted to use established techniques. He made his objections very clear to me. Mostly his concerns were that technically, my ideas brought from the non-3D, non-IMAX world would not work out, for various reasons. But I kept challenging him, so we had some awkward and tense moments at the beginning.

As the film progressed, we would go to New York every weekend to see the dailies, there being no IMAX theatre in New Brunswick. From the dailies, I learned to recognize the limitations of the system, and I deferred to Noel and his instructions from there on in. He also saw that some of his perceived limitations could actually work. Ultimately this tug of war brought us together as close friends. The sad ending to this story is that I lost my dear friend Noel Archambault, whom I greatly admired and respected, when he was killed in an ultra-light plane crash while filming in the Galapagos.

Flatland

In 2002, I was offered to direct an episode for a television series being shot in China, produced by Andre Morgan and Al Ruddy, who had produced *The Godfather*. The series, called *Flatland,* was about a group of young Americans who visit Shanghai, get abducted, and then are taken to a place called *Flatland* by the mysterious Mr. Smith, played by Dennis Hopper. As I mentioned in an earlier chapter, this series featured Chinese wire work and acrobatics and a crew that worked at a dizzying pace. I ended up doing eight episodes for the show.

After I finished the episodes I had been contracted to do, the producers asked me if I would stay on to handle Dennis Hopper's first foray into television. His time was 'block booked', which meant all of his scenes in the twenty-one episodes were shot together, amounting to a schedule of three months. It was a tall order for me because there was a lot of research; reading all the scripts to figure out the chronology and how everything fit together. Dennis was a hero of mine from *Easy Rider* and *Apocalypse Now*. I knew it would be challenging but I agreed.

Dennis came onto the set on the first day of the shoot and had a four-page monologue to do. To say he was surly is an understatement; he did nothing more than growl single-syllable answers to any questions asked by me or the crew. The local Chinese crew, along with a fair number of Australians who had come in, were understandably tense, given his larger-than-life persona. I introduced him to the other actors and he was almost completely unresponsive; really cold.

When it came time for the first take of his monologue, on my "Roll camera, action please" instruction, he didn't know his lines and he was all over the map. The second take wasn't any better. I could tell that the other actors and the crew were starting to wonder, *What have we got here?*

I wasn't behind the camera on *Flatland*, which was very unusual for me, so my focus was only on directing. We did about four takes and he wasn't anywhere close to where he should have been for the scene. So I asked him "Dennis would you like some cue cards by the lens to help you with this long monologue," No

*In Shanghai with Dennis Hopper discussing ideas
for the Flatland series.*

it was asking a well-seasoned film actor if he needed a cue card. Dennis's face went all red and he screamed in my direction and, then he went into a big tirade swearing and yelling up and down at everything in sight, in particular at the script, the crew, and me – he gave supreme hell to all of us. As far as I was concerned, I wasn't about to leave until I had the scene. Fortunately the tension got broken when his assistant brought in his morning tea. On about take eight or so, he gave a superb performance. He had finally found out where to go with the monologue and it was pure magic. I learned a very valuable lesson from this great actor that sometimes it takes time for the actors to search and feel until they get a hold of the scene and when they do get a hold of it, they give a powerful performance.

The next few days, Dennis' attitude did not change. Most of the time, he was unhappy on the set. He hated the scripts and since it was his first foray into television, he was having a hard

*Getting in some R&R in Shanghai
with Dennis Hopper.*

time with the pace of work, which is quite different than the feature film world. Features, and especially studio features, tend to allow more time for prep, whereas television is much more of a grind. Meanwhile, I had to figure out how to spend the next three months with an unhappy star who I needed to get a powerful performance from. So I spoke with the producers, who were already aware of the problem, but there was no resolution. I did agree with Dennis about the scripts and even though I talked to the show runner about our concerns with the script, my efforts were ignored. It was a difficult time for me, I didn't know how I could deliver something to the producers that they could make sense of, given that the star was so unhappy.

Dennis was always on set half an hour before call time and so was I. So I took that opportunity to meet him one morning for tea. I asked him, "Dennis, how many films have you done in your career?" He responded, "I don't know, maybe a hundred."

your career?" He responded, "I don't know, maybe a hundred." Then I said to him, "How many scripts of those films you thought were great?" and he answered, "Most of them sucked." My next question was, "How many films have you done then where you felt that you did good?" He looked at me like what the hell are you talking about. He answered, "Maybe three-quarters of them." I spun it back to him, calculating the logic of the situation and said, "You said you've done over a hundred films and that the scripts were all horrible, but you just told me that over three-quarters of the performances you gave you feel good about." He shrugged and I carried on, "That's what we all do – take something, make the best of it, and make something interesting out of it. That's our challenge and payoff." He could not answer me back with anything more than a grunt and a snarl but we worked together well for the next three months. He threw a big party at the end and I remember him toasting me happily in his scruffy way, "I'm glad this fucking thing is over but I'm glad this guy was along with me."

Working with Actors

The Dennis Hopper story is only one example of ways to unlock an actor's best performance, be they male or female. Working with actors is one of the most crucial elements for directors, but because I had no experience in theatre or any such training, I also don't have that strength of an analytic mind which at times is needed to go deeper into the characterization. My experience differs as a result of my training from years of looking through the eyepiece.

Each actor has his or her difficulties that come from their own pressures they face for the screen so you need to give them any cushion you can. Acting looks easy but in reality, it is difficult work; God-given talent helps but isn't everything. Along with the pressure there is often a lot of thinking that goes on. Some actors like to dissect the scene from every possible angle to be clear about what may work, and there are other actors who say, "Vic, I don't want to talk about it." They just do it and see how it feels. I am like the second group; not as interested in how I 'think' as in how I 'feel'.

Coming from cinematography into directing, I am very aware

of the emotional connection between the camera and the actor. From behind the camera, I want the honesty of the actor on an emotional level because I rely very heavily on the visual sense of films rather than the dialogue. Most actors go the other way because they start with the dialogue. For me, it is what the actor does, not what he or she says.

In our Western culture, there's a lot of thinking and dissecting that goes on in the actor's process, particularly the back story, motivation and the uniqueness of their character. Some actors prefer to have an analytic sense of their character but then there are other actors who only want to know what you need them to do in a physical sense for the camera as opposed to the analytical sense. My job as director is to take the actors to a place where they express whatever the script calls for effectively with a moving performance. In my case, coming from the cinematic end of the spectrum into directing, I'm very conscious of what I need to see on camera. I feel fairly confident in what I need to see on the screen but how to take the actors from wherever they are to that, sometimes is not as easy for me. Finding the balance between the two has been my challenge for a long time. Over the years, I have learned much, and this learning will continue to the end.

Left Behind (2002)

Left Behind was based on a best-selling sixteen-book series of young-adult Christian books by authors Tim LaHaye and Jerry B. Jenkins. The series is about The Rapture in the Christian faith where true believers in Christ are taken instantly to heaven, and the rest of the world is left behind in chaos. In 2001 a couple of Christian businessmen in the States acquired the rights to the books, put together a budget for the series, and started shopping around for someone to make it. They took it to Hollywood and producers there apparently liked it but had a problem with these two guys not knowing much about filmmaking but still wanting production control, so Hollywood passed on it. Finally they found a small company here in Canada that had done a few Christian films, so the two original producers from the States and the two Canadians made a deal to team up and co-produce the film.

One of the American partners had seen *Cold Comfort* and asked me if I would like to work with them, to direct *Left Behind*. It was a very ambitious film with a story involving miracles, discoveries of Soloman's temple, big scenes at airports with planes, the Rapture, and attacks on Israel – in all a huge film. Then they brought in an executive producer who was also a Christian evangelical, so there were five Christians on the show and me, a non-Christian.

When the executive producer came on board, I was summoned to make my pitch and was asked why I wanted to do this Christian faith-based film when I am not a Christian. I met them and explained that I had grown up with no faith, but at the same time, like my father, I respected every faith. To me they all had the common goal of making you a better person and helping to find peace of mind. I said I didn't know much about the Christian faith or the Rapture, however, if as an 'outsider' I could be convinced to consider becoming an 'insider', then it would be a good film and that was my goal. They obviously liked my explanation and I started the film soon after.

Left Behind was a very ambitious film – it was budgeted for $6 million USD, though, at the time, I thought that the screenplay, as written, needed closer to $10 million. As we stared to prepare the film, the budget kept going down; practically every morning during prep I was summoned to meet with the Canadian producers with one theme – bring the budget down. There was a lot of pressure on me to make a good film but with a constantly shrinking budget. Finally, just before we were going on camera, the budget was settled at $3 million USD for production. This caused me many sleepless nights. Despite the money problems, Kirk Cameron, Brad Johnson, and Clarance Gilyard came in to act in the film and they gave good performances The design department in Toronto also did a fantastic job.

The truly innovative aspect of this job was that the producers decided not to release the film theatrically first but rather to go to a direct-to-video VHS and DVD release for the Christmas season and then go theatrically after Christmas. It was an amazing move because the *Left Behind* franchise was enormously loved

*Discussing tactics for performance with Brad Johnson
on the set of Left Behind.*

among Christians in America – millions of American kids had
been brought up on the book series. Almost three million copies
were sold on VHS/DVD and if you do the math, that comes out
big bucks in sales.

Subsequent to the marketing success, I got a call from the
New York Times and they wanted to know my thoughts on the
marketing techniques used to release the film. I remember saying to them that as long as people see the film, it doesn't matter how it gets to them. They were also very curious about the
budget because they'd heard conflicting accounts of how much
money had been spent on the production. I knew there were
discrepancies between the amount I had been working with and
the amount being announced by the various parties involved in
the media junket, so I deferred comment.

The film opened theatrically just after Christmas but as the
New York Times said in the article that was published, "Think

*Giving some subtle notes to Janaya Stephens
on the set of* Left Behind.

of its theatrical release as the crowning touch of a multimedia marketing coup." The production company tried picking up the franchise and did a few more of the books after, including one with Nicolas Cage, but the first one with Kirk Cameron was the most successful for sales.

Despite all the difficulties I was happy to do the film, however it turned out to be a film that also left a bad taste with me. Since I was a freelancer, I suppose I was obligated to serve the market, but I was lucky in that I had never had to do that before, working, as I had, for the CBC for twenty-five years. *Left Behind* was the kind of experience I never wish to have again. I have always been conscious of my own independence but it became even more of an issue because I was getting on in years and I had to ask myself if I really wanted to carry on making films in this kind of atmosphere. The answer was "No." Time is the most precious thing and so I went back on the path to follow my heart; first with *Partition,* and then with *A Shine of Rainbows.*

Chapter 8

Partition (2007)

WHEN I WAS AROUND EIGHT YEARS OLD, growing up in Kashmir, India, my father managed a movie theatre. This was a very prestigious job because people in the region loved movies and we always had people knocking on the door asking us if there was anything we would like them to do. They were, of course, hoping to get free passes.

The movie theatre was at street level and above the theatre was a flat where we lived. In the back of the flat there was a huge attic, which was really the roof of the theatre. I cut a small hole in the floor of the attic and from there I used to watch all the movies upside down; it wouldn't matter. When I'd hear certain dialogue or a song I loved, I'd run out to the attic – even during mealtimes – because I knew exactly what was going on in each and every movie. Thus began my love affair for the movies. I watched amazing chariot races, and cowboy movies like *Vera Cruz*, and adventures like *20,000 Leagues Under the Sea* and many classic Indian movies. It was magic and I wanted to be part of that magic at any cost.

While we were living in the apartment above the movie theatre, there was a handsome-looking Sikh gentleman, a close friend of my father, Mr. Singh, who often used to come to visit him. A few minutes later, a woman would come in wearing a Muslim veil, a black 'burka', as it is called. My father would say to me, "Go play," and it was obvious to me, even at that young age, that he was giving them some time to be together. Those days, just after the Partition of India, mixing the Muslims with the Sikhs was like mixing oil and water. They were two very strong factions and because of long-standing disagreements, had very little to do with each other. These groups would normally not even look at each other, let alone mix together socially – and yet, these two people were lovers.

One day my father, a very gentle soul who always had a happy nature, came home very upset. After my mother encouraged him to tell us what was wrong, he said, "Mr. Singh is gone." He went on to explain that Mr. Singh had gone with his lover, the Muslim girl, to the river and jumped into the swirling water below the dam. But for some reason, he got washed ashore. He came out and saw his lover in her black burka floating down the river in the distance, so he went back and took his life a second time.

That story stayed with me as a youngster, all these years. I thought, *Just imagine the love this man had for this woman that he took his life with her and then took his life a second time.* He wanted to be with her, living or dying.

So that was how the seed was planted in my mind that got me going on my film called *Partition*. I wanted to make it shortly after the success of the film *Gandhi*, which came out in the mid eighties, and I thought it would be nice to do a love story set during the time of the Partition. The film *Gandhi* was about the great man who introduced the world to the non-violence movement and persuaded the British to free India from their rule without firing a single bullet or bloodshed. However, *Gandhi* ends with the intense clash between Hindus, Sikhs and Muslims at the time of Partition. Overnight, the Partition of India created millions of refugees and thousands got slaughtered. There were also stories of love and compassion among this carnage.

I felt that this dark chapter of our history was unknown in the world except for the people of Southeast Asia. It needed to be brought forward.

I wanted to do this film right after *Gandhi* but that was unrealistic. I wrote a script treatment very fast but raising $10 million wasn't easy – I was a relatively unknown writer/director, the story took place mostly in Southeast Asia with World War

*On location in Northern India
for the shoot of* Partition.

II scene locations spread over three continents, and the script called for big scenes with steam trains, and huge crowds. A period film is, at the best of times, a hard sell.

There was difficulty with the money people from the very beginning. We had a great many meetings and knocked on many doors, without luck. I remember sitting in Hollywood with potential producers as they smoked their big cigars and heard them say, "We love your script, it's a good story and we gotta do it." Except one thing ... we can't have the hero die at the end, he has to live." I explained that the film was not about living or dying, instead it was about what we do when we do live. The noble stand my hero takes against hate is the essence of the film. What kind of footprints do we leave behind? I knew this explanation wasn't going very far with them.

I met with the same Hollywood producers a few weeks later and in the meantime had done some thinking about the plot and the principles. I said, "Guess what guys, you don't need to worry now, the hero is going to live at the end." They asked, "What do you mean?" and I answered, "You didn't want him to die so I'm going to keep him alive." The annoying part is that they were just full of hot air. Even after my compromises, they did not invest in the film; in fact we had no American money at all. There were times I was ready to walk away from it all, but time after time I was encouraged by others who would not let the project die. Everyone loved the original draft of the screenplay that I wrote and then Patricia Finn, who is a well-established film and television script writer, brought more layers and textures to my somewhat linear story, thus turning it into a stronger script

Over the time period we were working on the financing, Tina Pehme, Kim Roberts and I dusted off my company Sepia Productions to handle the production aspects of *Partition*. We finally got rolling on production in 2005, a full twenty years after I had first written the treatment. In the true spirit of the film, I cast people from all different racial and ethnic backgrounds, without concern about Muslims playing Muslims or Hindus playing Hindus, or that English would play the English. I wanted to just bring good actors and I didn't want to be labelling the performers, we are just people. Irrfan Khan, one of the top Indian actors of today – he was in *Life of Pi* and *Slumdog Millionaire* – is a Muslim and plays Avtar Singh, a Sikh; Kristin Kreuk, who did an amazing job as Naseem Khan, is Dutch-Canadian; and Jimi Mistry, who plays the lead, is Indian and Irish, was born in London, and was brought up a Christian. I did not want to stereotype by casting based on ethnicity or race because these people are actors and that's where the creative side of filmmaking expresses itself. (A bold move in this politically conscious world.) We brought in the fine Canadian actress Neve Campbell to play the character of Margaret.

No Good Guys or Bad Guys
There is a scene in the movie where a steam train pulls in, hauling slaughtered Hindus and Sikhs back into India from Pakistan. In the true story from history, Muslims slaughtered passengers

*Going over lines for a scene with
Neve Campbell who plays Margaret.*

*Working out some emotional moments with Jimi Mistry, who
plays the lead character, Gian.*

on a train and the train was sent back into India to teach a lesson to the Hindus. Only the engineer had been allowed to live. On the day we shot that scene, it was very hot and I had about 500 extras, all bloodied up by the makeup staff, ready to crawl up onto the train to dangle their bodies off the roof of the train cars and such. While this setup was going on, the assistant director told me there was a problem, which came as a shock to me because we had to get this all done in one day. He told me that the local people who had been recruited as extras were agitated and wanted to shut down the production. They apparently thought we were skewing the narrative to show Hindus in a bad light. Their reactions were purely based on their own past experiences of movies that made assumptions about good guys and bad guys.

For a while, I was quite tense about what to do. This conflict seemed to be an almost impossible hurdle, especially since I did not have command of the local language and was in the middle of a pressure cooker of a hot day to finish the scene. I kept my massive concerns to myself and didn't say anything to our Canadian producers or my other Canadian crew members. I asked the AD to give me a megaphone and to gather up all the angry extras. I took the megaphone and even though my Hindi was rusty, I tried to say a few words to let them know I wasn't a complete foreigner. Then I spoke in English, and what I said was translated to them by one of the costume ladies.

> This film is not about a blame game. It is not a political film but a film which deals with the love of two people who cross the border with their heart. It is a love story. The essence of the film is that we are all the same – no matter what god we pray to. The film is a celebration of humanity and love. It is what both of the faiths preach, Muslin and Hindu. There are no good guys or bad guys   just people

Suddenly it was quiet. It might only have been twenty or thirty seconds, but felt like a long time. The power of crowds in India is very strong and I truly thought they were going to close

From top (film frames): Irrfan Khan as Avtar Singh,
Jaden Rain as Vijay Singh,
Kristin Kreuk as Naseem Khan and Jimi Mistry as Gian Singh.

*Neve Campbell's character Margaret Stilwell hugging her brother
Andrew, played by Jesse Moss, before he goes to war.*

down the production, until that moment. There were some
murmurs among the crowd for a short time and then the head
spokesman, an elderly Sikh farmer, started to explain how he
remembered the actual event in 1947. He recounted about how
he clearly remembered the same scene at the station when the
actual train pulled in with all the dead bodies from Pakistan. He
indicated he accepted my explanation and then complimented
our re-enactment of the scene. Looking back, I think the extras
wanted to be assured that we were not taking a side or branding
the Hindus and Sikhs as the villains. After my little speech and
the validation by their spokesperson, I am happy to say that the
crowd simmered down and we got back to work.

Challenges in Casting
Partition had to be shot eighty percent in Canada according to
the guidelines set out by Telefilm Canada, which was one of our

The mustard-coloured fields in Partition *were actually shot in British Columbia.*

major funding agencies for the film. So the big question was *How to make Canada look like India of 1947?* It was a challenge but my cinematography experience came to the rescue and we were able to create India in British Columbia. All the scenes in the mustard-coloured fields were shot here, as you will see above, as were the street scenes when the hero came back from the war. I was happy with most of the work we did here. Not one critic here or in India ever doubted the authenticity of the locations.

One of shots we did here in B.C., however, turned into a something of a nightmare. There was a scene of World War II where Jimi Mistry's character and Irrfan Khan's character get thrown into the muddy trenches, and their English officer drowns. We had two nights to film it all, with stunts and explosions all rehearsed and cued up. Jimi flew in from London, and Irrfan was booked to fly in from Mumbai but Irrfan didn't show up, and we couldn't find out where he was. The producers were panicking because we were scheduled to shoot the next day and we still had costume fittings and many other tasks to complete with the actors.

The sequence was going to cost us $150,000 because of the special effects, rifles, explosions, costumes, filling the trenches with water, and so on; it was a huge scene. So the producers said that we'd have to recast, and Tina Pehme found a Palestinian actor who had acted in few Hollywood films. His agent negotiated $40,000 for his role, which sounded to me at the time to be on the high side but as the producers saw it, we had no choice.

Now, I normally don't like casting anyone unless I meet them face-to-face because I need to see the chemistry – what they look like, how they sound, some sense of their mannerisms, etc. But the pressure was on, so I talked to the actor on the phone and he sounded totally wrong and I told him as much. Somehow he talked me into hiring him anyway, convincing me that he could come up to expectations because of his craft as an actor. He flew in from New York the next day and I took one look at him and I knew that he was completely unsuitable. I didn't buy for a second that he could take on the character of the leader of the Sikhs. I asked myself … *What to do now?*

I didn't tell anyone else on the set of my intentions – not even the producers or the actors – but I carried on and shot the entire WWII scene with the unsuitable actor, but all along keeping in mind that I would be replacing him. I planned shots for the entire expansive scene in such way that I could replace another actor in his shots with ease. In the meantime, after the day was done, the producers got a call from the unsuitable actor's agent in New York. I suppose since we had done a big war scene, the actor probably called his agent telling him that the big scene was done and he was set to go to India to finish the rest of the movie. I suppose his agent saw the opportunity and since his contract hadn't been signed yet, figured that he could squeeze out extra money. The agent told our producers that he would be signing the contract for $100,000 because that is what his actor client usually got rather than settle for the original amount of $40,000. Unknown to the New York agent, I had no intention to

*Jimi Mistry hiding in the shade of
the hot mid-day sun under a pink parasol.*

keep his client in the film. They thought they had us by the neck after shooting that expensive scene; a lucky break for us. Kim Roberts implemented his skills as a lawyer and found that since we hadn't signed the contract, we were able to let him go.

I went to India right after that, met with Irrfan, and confronted him about where he'd been and why he missed the shoot. He had some excuses, but we put it all behind us, and re-shot all his inserts for the battle scenes that I had originally shot with the fired actor.

To me, casting is a crucial aspect of a good film, along with a great story. If I have these two elements right, then the chances are I have the potential to make a decent film.

Intense Visuals

There is a scene in the film where our protagonist Gian, played by Jimi, becomes a Muslim so he can go across the border to

The cutting of Gian's hair scene that took place in a studio emulating the Jama Masjid mosque.

meet his wife and to do that, he has to visit a mosque where the imam cuts his hair and gives him blessings. I wanted to shoot this scene in Delhi, in the beautiful Jama Masjid mosque that is one of the biggest and most stately mosques in all of India. Well, you'll never see a Sikh in this mosque and I wanted to take a Sikh, with a turban and with his son, into the building. When I went to the mosque and made my request, there was tension among the Muslim imams who said I was asking the impossible because in the first place, it would not be fair to the Sikh who would obviously not want to come. I explained firstly that he was an actor, and secondly that it was a very strong scene in the film because here was a Sikh who would convert to Islam for love; the ultimate sacrifice, so to speak.

They finally agreed to let us come at a time in between the prayers and we could film it quickly. I didn't really need much time in the mosque because the scene of cutting the hair would

A glimpse of the over 35,000 people who turned up when we shot at the Jama Masjid mosque.

bc in a studio anyway, but I explained to them that I wanted to have people in the scene, otherwise it would not be as interesting, I wanted to show the courage of my hero and that what he was about to do was for love. It took us about six months to arrange everything for this scene before the actual shoot. It was a small scene where Jimi goes in with his young son and they stand outside the mosque and they watch and then they go inside. We had wanted a few people at the mosque, as I mentioned, but that day, over thirty-five thousand people showed up. As you see in the above photo, people spilled out from the courtyard of the mosque and into the street. There had been an announcement that we were going to be filming on that particular day so all these people showed up, some having walked for a long distance.

The same kind of intense visual occurred for me in the film when I had two steam trains in place for the final scene.

We needed two trains the way it was written, one coming and one going. Well, of course steam trains do not run anymore, trains in India are all electric, but they did have steam trains in a museum in New Delhi. I was shooting at a station in the Punjabi city of Patiala, which was about 300 km from there but – only in India – two trains were brought in for us all the way there from Delhi. The trains took about two weeks to arrive because there are no water stations anymore where the engines could be filled with water for steam; this all had to all be done by hand. The organizers were so invested in the story that they blocked the whole Patiala main station, diverting the regular trains to a third line to bypass the station for almost a week. The scene in Alberta with a steam train in *Bye Bye Blues,* took only one day but cost as much as the entire India shoot with two trains and tying up the station for almost a week.

When I was young, I avoided my Indian culture because I thought it was not forward looking. Now, I don't see it that way. I have been always open with my feelings and I enjoy good and open conversation. I now know where, in a sense, it has come to me. The portion of the *Partition* shot in India was the high-light for me. People were friendly and totally open to share any kind of feelings on any level, including, at times, very personal feelings. I fondly remember the open innocence of the people who you can talk to anywhere, even strangers in restaurants or at bus stops, and they will respond to you with total openness. I suppose I've acquired that – I haven't lost the open friendliness of being Indian, for better or worse. When one gets as much cooperation and interest as we had in India for *Partition*, it is fantastic. That, for me, is the joy in filmmaking; I feel alive when I am making something worthwhile and sharing the time with people I are happy with.

Quick Re-designs

There is another scene in the film where early in the morning, all the Muslim refugees travel across the border into Pakistan and get attacked by Sikh and Hindu riders. Our Muslim girl is travelling with her parents, who get killed, but she escapes into

*At the Patiala main station where the regular
trains were diverted to enable us to shoot.*

the bushes where she is discovered the next day. So, that's the scene we needed to do, but it called for a jungle and everyplace in India is packed with humanity now. It would have all been jungle in 1947 with peacocks and tigers; all gone now.

The organizers found a place about twenty kilometres away from where we were staying, but to shoot in the first morning light, we had to bring out all the extras, camels, horses, and bullock carts in the black of night. Transporting the extras in buses out that far into the jungle was also a big job. I was told that I was asking the impossible. They suggested I shoot the scene at sunset instead, but I know from experience that the light is completely different at sunset and if there are any holdups in the scene, it goes to black. In the morning if there are holdups, at least there is light, which is technically advantageous.

We needed a generator out at that location in the nighttime because it was not wired for power. Over 500 people had to be brought out there by about 10 p.m. and by midnight, they'd go for costumes and makeup, get haircuts, have their watches taken off, and all that kind of thing. Chris Zimmer was with us as an executive producer and he was supervising the generator so that all those things could be done. Not only the people, but the camels, cows, horses, and buffalo with their carts would also have to be transported and looked after. I'd gone out the day before with my crew and picked all the camera locations because I knew that once the light came up, we had to start shooting. I had learned my lesson, from *The Burning Season* shoot years before that, to be fully prepared with three camera locations when the sun comes up over the horizon.

I was expecting that since we had everything ready to go, the next morning we would simply work with the actors a bit and shoot. Problem was, I woke up at 3:30 a.m. and it was raining like hell. The monsoon hit early for some reason and I got a call from Chris Zimmer, who had been there all night saying, "Vic you can't shoot. There's water everywhere and open wires everyplace for the generators – we're going to kill somebody." Safety was our first concern of course so we cancelled the shoot and sent all the buses of people back to town. Of course they were being paid anyway, which was fine, but for us, the money was wasted. I told the organizers to keep the camels, horses, cows and buffaloes tied up and to keep a wrangler for them because it didn't matter to the animals if there was rain or not and we might get some shots yet if it clears up. But we were reminded that when it starts raining it rains for weeks so we sent the animals back too.

The way I work, I really care a lot about the budget. To me, every penny is important and every penny should show on the screen, not in my pocket. So losing this day's shoot meant several hundred thousand dollars. We had a meeting over breakfast in the morning and I added a couple of different scenes in the film. The structure of the film was redesigned so that our financial loss was not so colossal. We took Neve Campbell, Kristin Kreuk and a few other actors out to the village and were able to use the rain as an atmospheric feature for additional scenes.

Jaden and me on the set of Partition.

Tina Pehme along with Jaden and other cast and crew members at the Jama Masjid mosque.

Jaden Sarin, Tina Pehme, Kristin Kreuk, me,
Neve Campbell, and Jimi Mistry.

Most directors know how to think quickly when something like this happens, I am not saying I am the only one. Producers are the bosses but as a director, I also feel like I should be responsible to the production as far as the budget goes. It's a privilege to be given a budget to make a film. I have worked on many productions where if I was working as a DP and the director said we couldn't do something, I would find a way, so let's try and think outside the box. What a joy it is to be in this business where they give you money and then say, "Go make a movie." It's not a right, it's a privilege, and I cherish that privilege.

Jaden's Role

There is a charming story in the background of Partition that involves my son, Jaden. When I wrote the script I wrote a part for a young girl to play the daughter of our hero Gian Singh but we auditioned a great many girls and they were either over-acting or not be able to perform at all. If a child actor is not able to perform because of the limited time and circumstances, it can be a very cumbersome and costly affair for the production. Close to the start of the shooting schedule, I decided at the last minute to change the girl's part to a boy's and I told Tina that I was going to cast our son Jaden, who was three years old at the time, to play the part. Tina was reticent but I told her I felt good about it and suggested we give him a try.

The very first scene we shot with Jaden was at night in the rain. It was a scene where his mother had gone away and both he and his father miss her very much. The two-part scene started inside at a shrine and then progressed outside in the street, in the rain. We were all set up for the interior scene and then asked to bring Jaden in for the shoot. As soon as he came in and saw all the people, the camera, and the lights, he freaked out. He saw me and lunged at me crying, "Daddy I want to go home, I want to go home." It wasn't quite what I had in mind but I got at least easy crying for the scene. I kept the camera rolling and hoping I would get just a three second shot. It took bit of doing and I got the shot I needed, but the challenge then was how to get the longer scene of him crying outside the house in the rain at night.

We were shooting in Canada and the rain was cold, but since it was meant to be set in India, Jaden was only wearing a thin cotton shirt. I set up everything precisely before bringing him on the set and placed him at his given spot where the cameras were set to roll. I lay down on the floor beside him, comforting him a bit but also holding onto his little feet so he wouldn't run away. Jaden cried, cameras rolled, Jimi was all rehearsed and knew what he had to do, we did a couple of takes, and Jaden's crying was just perfect for the scene. While we did this scene, Tina and the producer watched the scene from a distance and being his mother, was upset. I also felt the apprehension among the crew and our lead about Jaden – *How was it going to work out for the next six weeks with this child?* I am sure they would have voiced their disapproval but couldn't, as he was the son of the director.

That night, Tina insisted that we re-cast because she felt it was not going to work with Jaden. I didn't sleep all night because I felt that Jaden was perfect; he wasn't acting, he was just giving honest emotions. I argued my point that I wanted to keep him,

Tina agreed to give him another chance, and as it turned out, he didn't cry again and was the most cheerful person on set. Neve used to perk up every time she saw him and he became everybody's mascot. He had his own little trailer and would say, "Daddy, when can I go to my trailer?" Then he travelled with me to India and it was so nice to have him along. We did a half-hour "Making of Partition" special and when it was time for Jaden to be interviewed, we screened the scene for him where he was crying and his comment was, "Yes, it was very sad because my daddy in the movie was yelling at me." When asked how hard it was to make it look like he was crying he said, "No, not hard, because I was acting. I am an actor."

• • •

Partition opened on thirty-two screens in Canada, which was very good for us, and recognition by the ethnic communities has been a particularly important honour. There is a huge Sikh community in California too, and they embraced *Partition* as the feature film in their own film festival in 2010. The movie went to at least a dozen festivals, a lot of Muslim people attended at certain places, and that kind of acceptance makes my heart sing. To this day if I go to an Indian market to buy some little sweet I crave, I often have people recognize me and rave about how much they enjoyed *Partition* and how they appreciated that the movie showed equal respect for Sikhs, Muslims, and Hindus.

With respect to the distribution of the film, in Canada we don't have enough money for publicity for our productions. As an example, *Partition* played in a theatre in Vancouver and after a three-week run it was finally packing out, almost entirely through word of mouth. But just as momentum was building, the theatre pulled *Partition* because Hollywood had booked a Sandra Bullock movie that had ₡10 million for publicity, which goes a long way to attract an audience to fill the theatre right away. For *Partition*, we had $200,000. How do you compete with that?

I would like to see Canadian theatres reserve ten or fifteen percent of their screen time for Canadian films. If they could do that, we would have a foot in the door and Canadian audiences could be exposed to what they might like. That's one way to do it. Another way to build audience is for filmmakers to not make excuses like, "We didn't have the money," or "We couldn't afford Russell Crowe." If you need $20 million, then find $20 million and make it work at the box office. Or a third way is the Australian model. They are distinct and forthright about what kind of films they like and they speak their minds because they have developed their own sensibilities and character and they are proud of it.

Canada got caught between England and America. We're not quite American but we are not English either so we have developed a sort of a mental feeling where we are afraid to go all the way into entertainment like the Americans – totally unrealistic filmmaking most of it, but they totally choke your emotion and take you for a roller coaster ride. At the same time we don't have that kind of zany sense of humour like the English; nobody can do comedy better than the British. So we got caught between and that's why we have a poor identity in the film sense as compared to, for example, the Australians.

Chapter 9

A Shine of Rainbows (2008)

EARLY IN MY LIFE when I first left home and shared accommodation with a few other older boys in Melbourne, Australia, I was very impressed by their knowledge. They all had so much to say about everything. However, as the time marched on, I also realized that the smartness of these boys came from reading other people's opinions through books. From then on, I developed an aversion to reading other people's thoughts and knowledge, as I wanted to form original ideas rather than copying others. So I developed a phobia for books. I have read plenty of scripts, but I haven't read many books in my life.

That said, I did read a small story, though, by Lillian Beckwith, recommended to me by my ex-wife Diane, who said that I might like it. The story was beautifully written and I could feel the ambiance of being on the Isle of Skye. I'm a visual guy so it really grabbed me; I could feel and see the potential for a timeless film. That was in the late eighties and it stayed with me for over twenty years. When we finished *Partition*, some funders and others asked me what I wanted to do next and I told them about Lillian Beckwith's story, "Shine of the Rainbows."

The story itself is timeless and is a celebration of unconditional love. It is about a boy who is adopted from an orphanage by a colourful and enchanting woman and her curmudgeonly husband. It is set against the lure of the ocean and wildlife and is very magical and whimsical and, at the same time, very real. I am not well versed in Celtic culture, so I teamed with a writer

A spread, here and facing page of the sensational scenery of the north coast of Ireland used as location for A Shine of Rainbows.

who had a Celtic background, Catherine Spear, and together we wrote the script. When I write, I like to bring someone in with me because my English is not quite perfect. To raise money, a script need to be polished and first-rate. The producers felt the screenplay needed another set of eyes to take it further and a wonderful man and excellent writer, Dennis Foon came onboard for the final draft.

By 2008 we were travelling all over the world looking for locations. I wanted to get a small off-coast island in the middle of nowhere where there would be rainbows, seals, and rugged vistas with expansive scenery. I had thought of shooting in New Zealand, and then we thought about Nova Scotia or Newfoundland – we even talked about South Africa. And then Tina Pehme was on her way home from Sepia meetings in Europe and she stopped over in Ireland because the Irish Film Board was pitching their locations to producers. Tina had a chance to visit a location in the far north of Ireland and when

she came back, she said, "I think this might work, you should take a look."

I went over with the assistance of the Irish Film Board to meet Aideen Doherty from the Donegal Film Office, Northern Ireland. Aideen picked me up from the Belfast airport and we drove on the narrow country roads surrounded by sheep, deep green grass, and an amazing sky covered with fast-moving, low-hanging clouds. It was my first trip to this part of Northern Ireland and I loved it. The journey took us right to Malin Head in County Donegal and through the car window way below and off to the side, I saw a deserted beach. There were low-hanging clouds all around us thus casting heavenly streaks of sunlight everywhere; a feast for the eyes and a treasure for the camera. This dramatic shifting light looks great but often is difficult when you're making a movie. Film scenes often take time to shoot and it is difficult to match light in the scene when it keeps on shifting and changing. However, I prefer this to the security of flat

Connie Nielsen in
A Shine of Rainbows.

lighting. Aideen, in her lovely Irish sing-song accent, said that this was just one of the places she wanted me to see but I told her, "This is just great. We'll use this location."

Aideen laughed and said, "No lad, I know it is great but you cannot film here. The weather changes constantly and it is very windy up here. You can hardly stand, never mind filming. That's why no film has been shot here before. As she was talking, I took out my still camera to take a few photos for the art department. I couldn't even open the car door, the wind was so strong and howling. Aideen had a great laugh – kind of like *I told you so.*

I was firm with my decision and Malin Heal was the precise location we chose for the film. The very first day of filming, we started on the same very spot I saw with Aideen, and no one believed the calmness of wind that day – a magnificent start for our small journey.

The Irish Film Board came on as a co-production funder and in combination with our Telefilm money, we had a total of about $7 or $8 million dollars. Keeping in mind the warnings about

Aiden Quinn in
A Shine of Rainbows.

the weather, I had the interior cover set of the cottage built in a studio close by. Our thinking was that some days it might be too windy or rainy and we would have to move inside to stay on our schedule. It cost us about $30,000 to build the cottage, but we never had to use it even once, because the weather was absolutely perfect for the entire weeks of the shoot. The locals said that they had never seen that in their whole lifetime. There was a scene in the film where we needed rain, so I asked the production manger to make sure that rain bars would be available when we needed them. My Irish friends with their pea caps and cigarettes hanging from their lips chuckled and said, "Don't worry about that lad, you're going to get plenty of rain each and every day of your shoot." During the entire six weeks, it did not rain for a single day and I had to bring in artificial rain bars, all the way from Dublin.

The Irish are very union conscious and are also strong in enforcing rules on any production. I chose County Donagal partly with that fact in mind, thinking that I would be able use

John Bell as Tomas, Tara Alice Scully as Nancy,
and Jack Gleeson as Seemus.

the local fishermen and others to give me hand with the water scenes, which we had plenty of in the film. I had never intended to bring in union people for the water safety, stunts crew and so on from Dublin. The Irish are also very strict about how many hours a child can be on set. John Bell, who played the boy Tomás in the film, was under ten years old and was in every scene. Normally we work twelve hours a day but since John was only allowed nine hours a day, we opted for French hours, which means there is no break for lunch – you eat on the set. We tried to convince the local guys to do French hours but they wanted their break for lunch and midmorning breakfast with bacon and eggs and they resisted, but finally we talked them into it. At the end of the shoot they complimented us about how smart it was because they all had their evenings free. In our system in North America, when you are working on a movie you just go to sleep and back to work. This way the crew had a life after work and we'd be in the pub together in the evening and happy to be back to work in the morning.

John Bell as Tomás *with Smudge, the seal
in* A Shine of Rainbows.

Besides John Bell, who has gone on since to play more grown-up roles like Spud in *T2 Train Spotting*; playing the boy Seemus, we had Jack Gleeson who went on shortly after to play Joffrey in *Game of Thrones*; and Aiden Quinn, the great Irish-American actor who'd been in *Bury My Heart at Wounded Knee* among a great many other roles. For the lead actress's role we were looking at Connie Nielsen who was Danish and had been in *Gladiator* and *Rushmore*. She'd read the script and liked it so I flew to LA where Connie was at the time, but when I met her, she had a very strong Danish accent. Despite her insistence that she would get the Irish accent right before we started shooting, I had some doubts, as I'd had some negative experiences with that very thing. Also, Irish accents and dialect are very distinct and difficult and the Irish are sensitive about their various dialects. Ireland is a small country but every fifty km or so you will find a new dialect.

We drafted up a script variation that had a backstory of Aiden Quinn's character bringing back a wife from Denmark,

*With the camera, looking out over
Dunluce Castle, built in the 13th century.*

but Connie wouldn't agree. She still insisted she could get the accent right. And she did! Just like what Meryl Streep is famous for. Connie came to the set speaking with a perfect Irish accent and used the accent for the whole time we were shooting, on and off the set. She was so convincing that the locals thought for sure she came from County Donegal. That is a story of true talent as an actor.

After the main unit shoot, we had almost no money left to finish the film and we still had to film a few crucial scenes with the young actors. I tried to pare down the number of the crew members needed for the scenes to accommodate the budget but it didn't go over well with the Dublin-based crew. They were sympathetic but would not make any compromise or concessions in their rates and the number of people they would bring in for those scenes.

We had no choice but to wrap the main unit and send them back to their home base in Dublin. We had finished everything with our two stars except there were still a few scenes left to do

Family meal scene with John Bell, Aiden Quinn, and Connie Nielsen in A Shine of Rainbows.

with the young actors. They were not complicated scenes but were crucial to successful completion of the film. The producers and I then created a second unit to finish the film using the parents of our young actors, along with a few members of our staff who we flew in from Canada. None of them had any experience of working on a film set, but everyone rose to the occasion and it was amazing how well they all pitched in. The scenes inside the cave and the scene when young Tomas is alone in the open sea rowing the boat with his seal, Smudge, are ones we did as a second unit.

• • •

For me, the real joy of making a film is the reaction of the audience. I am always interested to know at what point in the film people will cry, or laugh, or will be just plain bored. I am much more interested in what audiences think and feel about the film rather than what the critics say. What interests me is how an average person is touched or not touched – hates it or likes it.

Over the years I have attended a great many film festivals throughout the world and I attend these festivals to listen to people and learn about what they see and feel in the film. It is not for ego, but rather to have a conversation with people about what they think. When *Partition* screened at festivals, for example, people have said to me, "The film is so beautiful because I am married to a Muslim woman and we sometimes encounter discrimination," or "I want to marry a Muslim woman and the families are denouncing us. I want to show our families this film so they will find understanding." It excites me to think that my film is making a difference to some.

A Shine of Rainbows is really a story about unconditional love of a mother for her son. We screened the film at the Toronto International Film Festival (TIFF) and at the end there is always a Q & A period. You get about a half an hour if you lucky, and I saw a hand go up but we ran out of time and I wasn't able to get to the woman's question. I found the women in the lobby later, with a girl who appeared to be her daughter. I apologized that I wasn't able to get to her question earlier but told her I was all hers now. She said, "Mr. Sarin, I watched the movie and you have changed my life." She went on to say that she and her daughter had been having a difficult time, had fought and not seen eye-to-eye but that was now behind them. She came to realize what was most important in her life, and that was her daughter. She said, "She is my baby and that is my life now." The girl standing beside her started to cry, then the mother started to cry, and that little experience made me think why I love the movies and want to be part of them. There are many stories like this and I cherish every such moment.

Later that year, I received an invitation to attend the Shanghai International Film Festival with *A Shine of Rainbows*. I know China quite well because I had lived in China for about a year and I asked the festival organizers how much time we had for Q&A at the end. They said, "We are just happy to see you, thank you for coming," which indicated to me that they did not have a Q&A. I thought to myself *What? You brought me all the way over from Vancouver just so I could watch my own movie? That doesn't make sense.* I told them that I had come over to talk to people because I wanted to hear the Chinese audience's views on the film but they told me flat out it was not possible. The film screened, the film finished, and as the credits rolled before the lights came up, I went right straight to the interpreter's microphone and I said to the audience, "Hold it guys, nobody goes yet. I've come a long way and I want to talk to you. Please talk to me."

There was no response from the crowd. They didn't know what to do so I spoke for a few minutes. Everyone, especially the organizers, were embarrassed and it was a very awkward situation but I made a genuine plea to the audience that I was not about to leave until they spoke out about their impressions. Then slowly one hand went up in the audience, then the second and the third and we had a very good dialogue about the beauty, positivity, and the relationship between the mother and the child. The conversation we had broke the ice and I remember a couple of guys coming up afterward, hugging me, and saying, "You made me cry, you bad boy."

PART III

The Present

and Beyond

Chapter 10

Documentaries: the Reality of Life

DOCUMENTARY AND DRAMA, OR 'FICTION', are two very different concepts of filmmaking; they're both satisfying and fulfill their mandate to provoke emotion in people, but on different levels. The power of film, fiction or documentary, is so strong, that when the audience watches, you'll see them cry, or they'll laugh or sometimes even get angry. When you move people's minds and hearts from a moving image or from a scene, the power is wonderful to see. Documentary and fiction are quite different in execution. With fiction films, I recruit the help of actors, musicians, editors, and by having everything under control, I can push emotional boundaries. Documentary, on the other hand, teaches us the honesty and reality of life.

We often point fingers about the ills of the world at others without ever thinking that *Hey, maybe I am part of the problem.* Over the years, I have seen a huge shift in political correctness throughout the world, particularly among Western countries. It's ironic that we profess how democratic we are with the freedom of speech and so on, and yet we are afraid to speak our minds. In my documentaries, I am not afraid to go head on with tough subjects, with honesty. At the same time, especially now as I grow older, I feel that one needs to look for hope as well. If subjects are all doom and gloom, then what is the point of living? It is important to me to be honest with the subject but at the same time to have an anchor of hope and even celebrate the beauty of our world.

I did my very first ten-minute colour documentary *Endless Cycle* soon after I arrived in Canada in the early sixties. I didn't have any money and film stock was expensive, not to mention the processing so I begged favours from cameramen who were working in the news department of the CBC. They would let me have the short ends of unexposed film stock they hadn't used or didn't think was worthwhile to keep. People at the film lab were also kind to me and they would sometimes process my film either for free, or with a discount.

My *Endless Cycle* documentary was just a simple story of the cycle of seasons; no dialogue, only visuals in colour using Niagara Falls as a metaphor for the cycle of life, contrasted with the cycle of nature. While my friends were enjoying weekend parties or outings to Cottage Country, I would take my little Bolex camera and drive up to Niagara Falls. I must have done a couple of dozen trips in all to capture the Falls in different seasons.

Every penny I'd saved went into finishing the film and I was delighted when my little film was purchased by CBC. Back then, small film fillers were often used between television programs, because there were far fewer commercials those days and sometimes no commercials at all. It was a great high for me as a young filmmaker to see my work screened on television, and the compliments and comments I received served as a road map for generating more ideas for documentaries.

Since then, every documentary I've ever embarked on has taken me from knowing nothing about a topic to having a new door of knowledge open to me. I'm not looking for a great story in a documentary, I'm looking for an idea, and then I go and open that idea and discover what's there. If you have a great story, anyone can make a film. The challenge is to allow an idea to unfold, and see where it takes you on an unknown journey.

Following the unknown path is what I thrive on. Something I insist on for my own style of documentary is that it not be contrived. The fun thing in life is discovery, on any level — if I know exactly what I'd be doing with the rest of my life, it would not be nearly as interesting. Or if I climb up a mountain and already know exactly what is up there, it will never be as exciting as rooting these treasures out without knowing they are there. Not knowing and then discovering is the greatest joy.

When I work on a documentary, I don't need a large number of people along with me, I can just take my camera and off I go. There isn't the pressure of all the crew members and all the money – the process is more relaxing and I can enjoy the process of discovery. I am probably one of the few people in Canada who does films on my own, basically not waiting for someone to give me money. Mostly, I spend my own money, and I love it.

Solitary Journey (1989)

While I was in Kathmandu, Nepal in 1968 working on the *Children of the World* series, we took a small, light plane to capture footage of Mount Everest. We flew in from the plains and gradually the altitude built up as we climbed up through the valley of mountains – 10,000 feet, 12,000 feet, 14,000 feet, 16,000 feet – building up until at the end of valley, we saw Everest looming above us at 29,000 feet. As we were flying closer to Mother Goddess Everest I saw, to my surprise, Sherpa villages higher than us and children running along the edges of mountains, waving down at us. This was a sight I will never forget as long as I live; I felt the power of the Himalayas, the power of nature, and the incredible strength of Sherpas.

At about this same time, I was intrigued by the idea of celebrating 'Number Two's' 'Number One's' we all know, but it was my impression that for every successful event or successful person, there is someone behind it doing a lot of the work; the 'Number Two's.' As a way of exploring this intrigue I had with Number Two's, I fixated on the Sherpas in Nepal and I wanted to do a documentary film about them. Sherpas, after all, helped all the climbers to scale Mount Everest over the years. The Sherpas themselves can go up and down without too much problem, and without the Sherpas, the famous explorers would not have been able to complete the climb, particularly in the old days.

I talked to a number of people and I met with discouragement. They'd say, "Are you crazy? BBC has already done two films on them," or "What are you doing differently than what

With Dawa Tenzing and his Sherpa friend
in Nepal for Solitary Journey.

National Geographic Channel has already done?" That type of reaction does not bother me because as artists, we feel and see things differently and our films will be different as a result. It's a personal take, from our souls. Hopefully someone who sees the film will like it and will get something special out of it.

I asked a couple of my friends to come on an adventure to Nepal, saying, "Let's go to Nepal and do a film on Sherpas." They didn't know anything about Nepal and they were very excited to experience it. So we went to Nepal and I found Dawa Tenzing, a Sherpa who was eighty-two years old at the time and who was with Edmund Hillary and Norgay Tenzing – as a 'coolie' as they used to be called – on their expedition to the top of Everest in 1953. The expedition leader had been John Hunt. As part of my fledgling documentary, I arranged interviews with both John Hunt and with Dawa Tenzing – the top dog and the guy at the very bottom.

Photo: Scott Eldridge

*With Suzanne Cook and Dawa Tenzing,
a Sherpa who was on the first Everest climb.*

*Nepalese Children wondering about the
camera we had set up.*

I met with Brigadier Henry Cecil John Hunt at his gin and tonic club in London, and as a first interview question I said, "Sir Hunt, why did you climb Everest?" I could see his English mind being very polite while at the same time thinking *What a stupid question to ask*. "Well," he said in his plummy accent, "because we simply had to climb it. It's the highest place on Earth and we had to conquer it." Interesting, I thought, all right.... I asked him a few more questions then flew back to Nepal and met with Dawa in his hut, Mount Everest looming behind us in the distance. I asked him, "You were on that climb, but why didn't you climb Everest on your own?" Rolling through my mind were the thousands of people who come to climb from all over the world and all the time and money they put into training – even occasionally falling to their death. I carried on with my question to Dawa saying, "You Sherpas go up and down, why weren't you the first up there? Didn't you want to conquer it?" He laughed, and laughed, and laughed some more, and would not stop laughing. When he calmed down, he leaned toward me and said, "Vic, I have to climb my inside Everest first before I climb the outside."

I had my focus, and from there my whole film was based on what there is to climb. The Western attitude is that everything has to be conquered. The Eastern attitude is no, one has to purify oneself first. *Solitary Journey* is an example of going into a documentary project totally open and discovering an idea. The film was very popular, winning an unprecedented three-award sweep at the Banff Mountain Film Festival along with thousands of dollars of cash in prizes at many other national and international festivals. In addition to the awards and prizes, with *Solitary Journey*, I came to realize that everything has been done before and that we see the same idea in our own unique way. I have never been anxious that an idea is not new – it is always a matter of how you see it. If an idea interests you, go for it.

Desert Riders (2011)

In Dubai and Saudi Arabia in the Middle East, there is so much affluence they sometimes don't know what to do with it. The biggest sport they have there is camel racing; to them it is like

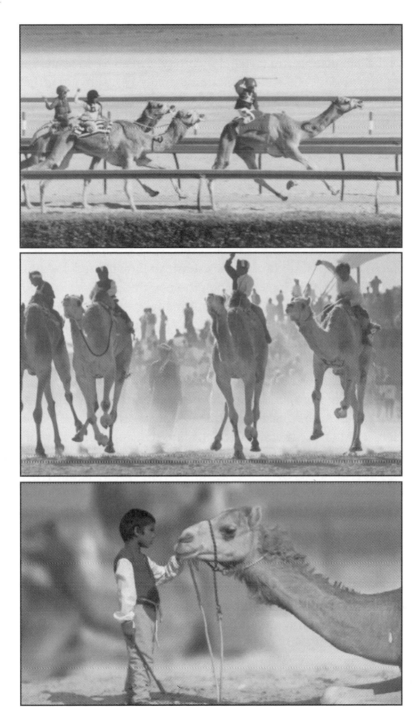

Frames from Desert Riders.

hockey is to Canadians. To keep the camel jockeys light-weight so the camels can run faster, they brought in children as young as three or four years old from impoverished Muslim countries like Bangladesh, Pakistan, Mauritania, and Sudan. By the end of the 1980s there were as many as 40,000 children looking after the camels and riding in these races. Word had it many of these boys were also molested and sodomized. A lot of the kids died and they'd bury them in the sand, right there – they didn't care.

Bruce Cowley, the head of the Documentary Channel came to know of this sad story and contacted Naomi Weiss, a successful producer in Toronto to see if she would be interested in taking a look at this problem. Noami set out to find a director who would be suitable to take on this sensitive film, offered it to me, and I took on the challenge, with the condition that she would come up with evidence that these atrocities were actually occurring. Naomi found a crusader for the cause who was trying to save these children and who had some actual footage of these kids riding camels and talking about the abuse. Once I saw the evidence, I knew we had a film.

Partly as a result of *Desert Riders*, the child slavery in Dubai and Saudi Arabia has practically stopped. There were other elements that went along with our film to bring about the end of using children as jockeys, but I feel good to say that the film helped. Now that children are banned from riding the camels in races, little remote-control robots ride instead, operated by the camel owners. (Mind you, the robots are still dressed to look like little people.)

More than anything else, I like to do documentaries to lift the human spirit and give people strong values of humanity. We have been very much a consumer society; everything is based on economy and economic growth. How far can you go with growth? What about the richness of your own soul? I hope that through my films, people will become more concerned about being honest, having integrity, having character, and respecting others. I am gravitating towards this lately because I am in my last lap in life. My hope is that I have changed some people's perception of what is important in life.

Frames from Hue: A Matter of Colour.

Hue: A Matter of Colour (2013)

The National Film Board was good enough to ask me if i would like to do a film for them so I proposed a couple of ideas including *Hue*, which they went for. I put the principle of *let's see what we find out along the way* in place years later with *Hue: A Matter of Colour*, much as I had with *Solitary Journey*.

I don't like hypocrisy, which there is a lot of among the human race as a whole. The ethnicity I come from, the brown race, can be very hypocritical when it comes down to the shade of their skin. The Indian people are more conscious of colour than any other people on this planet. Throughout the history of mankind, lightness has always been in demand and globally, multi-billions of dollars of skin-lightening products are sold every year, notably in India, Philippines, Thailand, and Africa. In India, for example, in the same family, the child with the lighter skin is often favoured over those with darker skin and for that reason, might have a brighter future. That principle has been reflected for hundreds of years in the well-established caste system in India. I wanted to explore this problem and that is what *Hue* is about.

Before doing *Hue*, I knew colourism existed but to what extent, I did not know. When I met a woman in the Philippines who made a huge business out of skin whitening, and when I met a lady in South Africa who married an Indian man and how much pain and hurt it created with her siblings, I began to understand the extent of colourism and its hypocrisy.

In all the documentaries I make, I like to hit the topic head-on with honesty, and I also like to give some hope and anchor some meaning at the end. In *Hue*, a Brazilian street sweeper was able to make something of his life. He's a big star in Brazil now; he opened the 2014 Olympics with his dancing, in spite of his dark skin colour. It's inspiring to know that we all can do that. *Hue* is a serious film in one sense, an honest film, but is inspiring at the end, as in don't let this stop you. It didn't stop him. It hasn't stopped me!

As a side story, The National Film Board liked the subject I was working with, but they insisted that I be in it so it could become my personal story. I didn't feel it was necessary, but political correctness is very strong in the world now, so I went along with it. I felt that by placing my family and myself into the film, the Film Board would probably have less to worry about if there were any controversies resulting from taking on this highly charged subject material. If there was to be any heat, the answer could be, *Well it is a personal story of one filmmaker ... this is what Vic wanted to do.*

*Andrew Holmes, Austin Andrews
and me, with Adam Robert, the boy from Geita.*

The Boy From Geita (2013)

When I did *Hue*, a storyline came through about albino people
in Tanzania who are persecuted because they have white skin.
Albinos are known there as 'zero-zero people' as if they are not
even human. It threw me off because my story theme from *Hue*
was completely opposite. When I got into the subject, the more
horrible I realized was this practice of oppression against albinos. In the year 2010 when I was doing this film, I could not
believe as humans we were able to go the moon and here we
were in East Africa killing people for body parts.

Peter Ash, founder of an organization called 'Under The
Same Sun', facilitated the whole film and he himself has albi-
nism. He was featured extensively in the film and it was very
satisfying to hear him say that we had done a good job helping
people out. He said, "Vic, this film has done so much good for
us. The killing of albinos hasn't completely stopped, but it has

slowed down and there is a lot more pressure to do something about it. But more than that, the local people are becoming more focused and educated."

There seems to be a tide turning where people in East Africa are saying, "These atrocities against albino people are horrible and intolerable." Meanwhile, through the efforts of people like Peter Ash, albino people in Africa are starting to enter more into the mainstream. In fact, in *The Boy from Geita*, we show how a Tanzanian albino Salum Khalfan Barwany, was elected as a Member of Parliament. When you educate people, the stigma diminishes, and we can see that Geita has made a huge dent toward giving the albino population equal rights.

The National Film Board of Canada (NFB)

I respect the National Film Board in the same way that I respect the CBC – because I have worked with so many good people from both places. Things have changed, though, with the NFB and it is worth a mention.

Going back in history to the 1950s, after WWII, things were nice here in Canada (I am assuming but I wasn't in Canada for most of that time mind you). Life was easier, people were positive and uplifted. These were the Golden Years for both the NFB and the CBC. The reason the NFB was able to bring so many people forward in the arts is because they encouraged artists at that time to go ahead and just do their own thing. It was a place that would support you but you could be fully on your own, so we were always independent as artists and creators. When you talk to filmmakers like Claude Jutra, Gilles Carle, and Don Brittain, they all learned from the Film Board because the Film Board was only there to support them, not tell them what to do.

That milieu is greatly changed now; committees do most everything. There are always ten steps before you can get anything done now. When I was doing *Hue*, NFB wanted me to give them a script letting them know what I was going to do. I said to them, "It's a documentary. I am going to go and doc-u-ment. How can I give you a script? I'm not doing a fiction." NFB used to hear your idea and if they liked it, they would support you to get

On location in the desert for a documentary shoot.
Alone with a small crew and my camera.

it done. In house, they had their labs and their editors and they would help you finish your film. In the fifties and sixties, that's why so many Oscars went to the National Film Board of Canada; because they were innovative and artists and creators were left alone. There are seven-and-a-half billion people in the world. We all look different, we sound different, and we also think differently so you can't make a movie by committee as in "Let's all talk about it." To make something interesting, you have to let one person do it and it is only that way you will find something of genius. Otherwise you're going to be doing mediocre work all the time.

Keepers of the Magic (2016)
Most of my professional career has been looking through the eyepiece of a camera and because of my intense relationship with the eyepiece, I have been fortunate to travel, meet amazing people, and witness some of the most interesting events of our time. This has brought me a very rich life on so many levels.

With George Miller, director of Mad Max: Fury Road,
at his studio in Sydney, Australia.

I often thought that I was overly compensated for what I did because it has brought me such great joy.

The most well-written screenplay, well-acted performance, well-designed set and all the rest can be completely powerless if the camera is in the wrong spot. On the other hand, a scene can come to life just by the use of one well-placed light and if the camera moves at the right moment, the actor becomes bigger than life. With the right use of colour in the frame, emotion can breathe into an otherwise flat scene. It took me many years to acknowledge a respect and pride in my work of looking through the eyepiece.

I have come to the conclusion that there will always be issues and difficulties in the world and it is good that we keep making films to address those issues. On the other hand, perhaps now that I am getting to run the last leg of my race, I wanted also to celebrate the contribution that film artists make to our world. My thoughts were, *What better way is there for me to express*

With the late Gordon Willis, cinematographer of The Godfather,
at his home in Massachusetts.

*something which is close to my heart than to celebrate my own
peers – the cinematographers.*

I've seen amazing films in my life; David Lean's films for
example like *Lawrence of Arabia, Bridge Over the River Kwai,
Dr. Zhivago, Passage to India,* and *Ryan's Daughter.* I adore all
his films because cinematically they are very lush, very big and
wide, bigger than life. When I saw Anthony Minghella's film
The English Patient for the first time, I didn't sleep all night that
night, I was so high. *The Last Emperor, Gandhi, Dr. Zhivago, The
Godfather,* and *Apocalypse Now* did the same thing for me. I felt
it was time to celebrate these cinematographers because people
don't even know what they do. That was the driving force, especially since 'film' is almost dead now; movies are all digital. I feel
that digital is a completely different world of photography, even
though people argue with me on that. Film was an art and it was
also a craft. It involved a lot more discipline and focus. So, as
for the awesome beauty and success of these films, I'm sure the

With Vittorio Storaro, cinematographer of Apocalypse Now, *at his home in Rome, Italy.*

cinematographers had a lot to do with it.

I became fascinated with knowing how these beautiful scenes came about. I wanted to talk to these icons, or masters, before they disappear because they are the only people who still have the knowledge and the magic of true film. That's almost gone now so I thought *Let's celebrate these people. Keepers of the Magic* is homage to great filmmakers.

I got along with all of these talented men very well; John Boorman who produced *Deliverance;* César Charlone cinematographer on *City of God;* Roger Deakins, cinematographer on *No Country for Old Men;* Philippe Rousselot, cinematographer on *Sherlock Holmes;* Bruno Delbonnel, cinematographer on *Amélie;* John Seale, cinematographer on *Mad Max: Fury Road;* Vittorio Storaro, cinematographer on *Apocalypse Now;* and Gordon Willis, cinematographer on *The Godfather* series. One of the reasons we got along, I guess, is because we are all old now. We exchanged listening and telling and I feel very proud of *Keepers.* The documentary that emerged about their lives and art had no story to begin with; I just wanted to celebrate, so we went ahead and allowed the story to develop as we went along. I'm pretty sure that *Keepers* will be a good museum piece for people who love cinematography. Gordon Willis is already gone – *Keepers* was his last interview – as has Haskell Wexler (*Who's Afraid of Virginia Wolf and Bound for Glory*) who had a couple of lines at the end of the film. These eminent cinematographers are slowly disappearing so I'm very glad I did the film when I did.

In the making of *Keepers*, I wanted to film these men sitting in their own homes, totally relaxed rather than on the set or behind the camera. So every time I went to see their homes, I told them to just go to a spot where they were comfortable and where the lighting was good and I would set up a camera. Not one of them would do that; they all want us to tell them what we wanted. They'd say, "No, that's your problem." I am assuming the reason for that was they were tired of making those decisions and thought, *let someone else worry about it for a change.*

John Seale, who shot *Mad Max: Fury Road, The English Patient, and Witness*, was a great case in point. He and I go back to my Australia days and he came in right after me at the Australian Broadcast Company (ABC). It was lovely to talk with him because we have the same sensibilities; like finding a twin. We also have Gordon Willis in the documentary who was very strongly opinionated but also very much a daredevil. Besides doing *The Godfather*, he did many of Woody Allen's films. Then you see Vittorio Storaro, who is very creative and very European.

Something I love about these masters is they bring their own cultural background into the work. European cinematographers are very much into the art and the way they use colour and their lighting is very painterly. Australians are totally instinctive and full of bravado, like I am (I can see my approaches to camera work come as much from Australia as from Canada). And then you have the Indian cinematographers who love colours and energy, as opposed to Ingmar Bergman and that Scandinavian era which is dark, and deep, and with no movement. South Americans like César Charlone are very political and they'll fight for their political ideals. Roger Deakins' work is very

*Bhai Ji, a fellow who runs a movie cart on
the streets of Mumbai, India.*

creative and he plays with light and darkness all the time, and much like David Lean's work, his scenes are wide and simple. I interviewed more cinematographers for the film but I only used seven, and the reason I used these seven is because their work is so well known. I wanted to be sure that the films that we talk about are ones that people remember. I would loved to have gotten Emmanuel Lubezki who won Oscars three years in a row for *Birdman, The Revenant,* and *Gravity,* but he was not available. The reason I wanted him was not only because of his excellent and innovative compositions, but also because he has now done a lot of digital work. I wanted to get his take on that side and glimpse his own creative process and challenges in that area.

• • •

When I did *Keepers of the Magic,* I shot a scene out on the streets of Mumbai with a fellow who runs a movie cart. Monkeys were everyplace there that day and dogs were running around but, apparently, nobody was feeding them. So I asked my fixer there, a young girl, "How do these animals live? There's no food even for people here, people are begging, how do the animals survive?" She said to me, "Sir, they do get food. A lot of Hindus, when they wake up in the morning, the first food they make they give to the animals, not for themselves." She continued to say that her mother would cook a couple of chapatis and the first chapati goes to the dog outside and then they eat.

I was very touched by this lovely gesture where every day they would share a little bit with the animals. I like documentaries that are directed to raise our consciousness, what's important in life. It's best if we can also make them entertaining because world problems keep coming at us all the time. Fifty years ago I thought that "Hey, after we do this film the world is going to be great," but holy smokes, the problems have never stopped and they never will. My goal now is to try to raise people's standards of humanity.

Chapter 11

Making Ends Meet

Back in the 90s, Tina Pehme was working as a coordinator on *The Burning Season* that I was shooting. She was a lovely, enthusiastic person, who was full of fun and could laugh at herself, which I thought was a fine quality. At the same time, she had very clear focus and a great love for the arts. I was very taken with her not only as a person, but also because of her abilities in the business, and I remember thinking I'll bet Tina will make a wonderful producer one day. I even told her to mark my words.

Tina and I started working together to develop films. She was passionate about *Partition*, a film that was, of course, very close to my heart. As I mentioned earlier in the *Partition* chapter, I originally developed the movie with Chris Zimmer, who I had worked with on *Margaret's Museum* and *Trial at Fortitude Bay*. In the late nineties, Tina began working with Chris to get *Partition* made. Subsequently she brought in Rose Lam who she had been working with on another film and they brought in co-writer Patricia Finn. The script for *Partition* went through modifications, and subsequently received positive attention, but was a tough film to make as it was period, and political, and set on another continent. Tina and Chris took another run at it and got very close and were about to start in preproduction in India when the financing fell through. It was a big blow after finally getting so close, so Tina and I put *Partition* on the back burner for the time being and decided to make another film first – something smaller and contemporary.

On location in British Columbia for
Deluxe Combo Platter *in 2003.*

The result was a romantic comedy called *Deluxe Combo Platter (2004),* starring Marla Sokoloff, Jennifer Tilly, and Dave Thomas, released in the US as *Love on the Side. Deluxe* proved to have its own set of hurdles and challenges almost every step of the way; for example our sales company went bankrupt ... twice! But it was a good start, and with Tina's help, I was forced to think outside the box to come up with multiple solutions logistically, financially, and creatively. Another lesson was that I should always have a plan B *(and C and D!).* It also taught me to the importance of finding like-minded people with complementary tastes and skills to collaborate with who shared the commitment to the vision both in production and on the financing side. It was on *Deluxe* that Tina began working with entertainment attorney Kim Roberts who became an integral member of the team and together we decided to take another run at *Partition.*

This time we were successful! With the support of the

The cast and crew from Deluxe Combo Platter
that was known in the US market as Love on the Side.

funding and talent agency relationships that we had solidified through the past few years, Tina, Kim and I were able to turn *Partition* into a reality. With the support of funders, distributors, broadcasters, and sales agents such as John Dippong, David Reckziegel, Shelley Gillen, Diane Boehme, Michelle Marion, Kirk D'Amico and Suzanne Jackson who became champions and collaborators with us in Partition and future films, we paved a road forward into our production phase.

It was in this configuration, Tina, Kim and myself, that Sepia Films moved ahead. Once completed, *Partition* did well for us on many levels but most importantly, it put Sepia on the map as a company comprised of filmmakers who could successfully make feature films on an international scale. We all brought our own strengths and weaknesses and together we covered different, yet essential sides of the filmmaking puzzle.

My contribution lies in the projects I am able to offer like *Partition* and *A Shine of Rainbows* and the documentaries that

I have been passionate about. Sepia is a very good combination of the three of us and our mandate over the years has evolved into a commitment to making films that have substance but also entertain and resonate with audiences all over the world.

Partition was a very challenging and satisfying project for all because of its period setting and location shooting in India and Canada and all of the pieces we had to pull together in order to raise the budget and put together a cast that meant something both in North America and globally. Similarly, making *A Shine of Rainbows*, as a co-production with Ireland, helped establish Sepia as a Western Canadian based feature film company that could successfully finance and produce international co-productions.

Films can take a long time to develop, especially when raising money, and we found we could not do everything ourselves. Sepia has grown to include a full time staff of approximately ten people, which, of course, expands exponentially when we are in production. It's a bit of a catch-22. You can't make interesting films or manage the development and production of multiple projects without enough supporting staff but you can't have enough supporting staff until you have enough money, which you have earned, to pay them. So it's a tricky path to follow. Tina and Kim were able to raise some financing but it's always a challenge, especially in the feature film model when so much time is spent in development (for example *Partition* took more than ten years) and there are no guarantees.

Exploring Television and the Nightmare Series
We decided to explore television as well, in order to create a sustainable business. As creative independent film producers Tina and Kim were only interested in making TV in the same way they made features, with material they creatively developed rather than service work. In 2010, through Kim, we were introduced to Meyer Shwarzstein, a lovely man who runs his own distribution company in Los Angeles called Brainstorm Media with strong US network connections. Meyer was also a friend of Shelley Gillen's who had been a huge champion of *Partition* when she was a Canadian broadcaster. Shelley was then forging

The Sepia team: Tina Pehme, Kim Roberts,
and me. Jasmine Sarin behind us.

a career as a writer and Kim, Tina, Meyer and Shelley began to develop TV ideas for various networks. Larry Gershman joined the development team through Brainstorm as well and the team hit home with *A Mother's Nightmare*, which was the first of the TV movies to be green lit.

Tina and Kim came to me and said they'd like to put my name forward as a director on this prospective film and I told them I wasn't interested. My initial hesitation wasn't because it was a television film – after all a film is a film and I had done a lot of quality television in my time – but because I knew television was more filmmaking by committee and I wanted to make sure I could bring something interesting creatively. I apologized to Tina but explained to her that I would rather carry on with my own documentaries because I needed to continue operating independently. She encouraged me to read the script anyway and she also assured me that my creative contribution would be valued and incorporated.

Top Left: A Mother's Nightmare (2012). *With Jessica Lowndes and
 Grant Gustin.*
Middle Left: A Daughter's Nightmare *(2013). With Emily Osment and
 Victoria Pratt.*
Bottom Left: A Sister's Nightmare *(2014). With Peyton List.*
*Top Right: With Natasha Henstridge, and with Kelly Rutherford on
 A Sister's Nightmare.*
Below Right: With Jaden Sarin on A Daughter's Nightmare
 (as Jaden Rain).

The script was good and came from a position of honesty. *A Mother's Nightmare,* is about a teen aged girl who takes revenge against her boyfriend who has broken up with her – a universal theme among teens everywhere. The story also touched on issues of mental illness, drug use, suicide, and peer pressure. As I say, I liked the honesty of the writing. This approach can sometimes backfire because it can become boring, but Shelley took enough chances with her writing and pacing to make it interesting. I thought it was a good script.

The problem then became that the network didn't know me, so Tina and Kim needed to introduce my work to them. I must say my ego was a bit hurt at the time but they sent my reel along to them anyway. The question that came back from them was, why would I want to do a TV movie when I had a background making features films such as *Cold Comfort, Partition*, and *A Shine of Rainbows*? I told them a film is a film, and that the material was good and for me the medium doesn't matter so long as I think I can do something interesting with it. I am at heart a film maker and I would rather be making films for television than solely developing features and only making one every few years or more. Like exercise, I think the more we get to practice our craft ,the more we bring to all of our projects, regardless of genre or medium.

When we started production in 2012, I suggested we shoot the film in Kelowna, B.C., which was a surprise to the producers. I told them that I wanted to have more time with the camera and more time with the actors which by now included Jessica Lowndes as the tormenting girlfriend, Grant Gustin and Annabeth Gish as the mother and son whom she torments. I had been thinking about the Okanagan to shoot in for several years, after having spoken at several film festivals and events there. The physical location is stunning, the residents are 'film friendly', and there is more room to move and breathe. We could also base all of our locations close to our hotel so there would be less time lost in commuting. I was able to convince Tina and Kim of Kelowna's merits for the physical production and from a financial perspective they did their homework and it made

*A favourite performer on
the* Mother's Nightmare *shoot.*

sense. We all had the common goal of elevating the look and feel of our television to give it more of a cinematic feature film quality, which Kelowna allowed us to do.

A Mother's Nightmare premiered to stellar ratings in 2012 on Lifetime, and became the first movie within the *Nightmare* franchise, on which we are now on number six. It helped to establish Sepia as a company that produced top quality product in the television arena as well and from there, other television followed.

In 2013, we went back to Kelowna again for production and Jon Summerland, who is the Okanagan Film Commissioner, has been a huge support and tremendous resource. It has been a real win/win relationship – Sepia has now shot eight movies in the Okanagan region and has helped to build the infrastructure there.

The *Nightmare* franchise has given us some breathing room to pay staff and to carry on with development of both features and other television. For me, I enjoy working on the movies but it has also provided me the financial means to pursue my own documentary work, which is a labour of love. I need to be busy and to explore subjects that I am passionate about while doing what I love the most – making films. Tina and Kim have expanded the TV division and gone on to develop and produce a diverse range of television productions such as *A Perfect High* (2015) with Bella Thorne, *Straight A's* (2016), and *Drink Slay Love* (2017) directed by Vanessa Parise. They have also had a chance to work with new partners such as Sheri Singer. The collaboration with Brainstorm has expanded to other networks such as Hallmark and The CW, starting with last year's *Summer in the City* that I directed. Television allowed Sepia to not only sustain itself, but to grow to the next level on the feature side. Tina and Kim produced the Argentina/Canada/Italy 3D feature *The Games Maker* and a 2017 feature, *Anthem*. The team has also grown from the contributions of a young film editor named Austin Andrews. Austin and I have worked on five or six films now together including these Sepia television dramas and my own documentaries. Austin also edited *The Games Maker* entirely in 3D and completed *Anthem*. He is like a mirror to me of what I used to be like at that age, so we connected right away. Like me, his passion is films 24/7. Austin has been a huge asset to Sepia and in particular to me.

A Practical Grounding

With Sepia having a grounding on a practical, business level, which we need to keep the machine moving and well oiled, I am able to take creative risks and explore themes that really matter to me, and that I deeply care about. A company like Sepia needs a base of revenue; that is the reality. Of course, my idea is to always make films that not only entertain but uplift society on some level so I draw the line at gratuitous violence. In my dramatic films, I think the world has enough of that and I would rather provoke thought, support themes of love and acceptance, and bring something positive to my films, if I can.

I can't imagine a world without films and even though a

huge majority of films do not make money, there are more films getting made – now more than ever – which tells me that film is a passion shared by many. One thing I have learned is that you have to be responsible about the films you are making, it is tough to get them out in the world and you have to really believe in what you are making to put in that energy and effort. And the team is key – to work with people you trust and share a sensibility and passion with is essential and makes the experience that much richer.

Chapter 12

Looking Forward

ONE THING I FEEL VERY HAPPY ABOUT is that I found Canada and Canada took me in. Canada is probably the best country in the world; not only because I have enough to eat and can stay warm, but because I am given the sense of freedom to do what I want to do. The 150 or so films I have worked on exist because of Canada and that, to me, is a wonderful gift. The sad part, though, is that I haven't been able to do much to pay back this country, which has been so good to so many of us. I've always wanted to make a film that celebrates this great nation.

I was born in one place, India, and grew up in another, Australia. But for the last fifty years, Canada has been my home. Because of my travels – first as a cameraman for the CBC, then as a filmmaker in my own right – I have a clear perspective and a sense of what Canada stands for in the world. When you speak to people in foreign places you learn so much about the place you come from. How people around the world see Canada is a constant reminder of how wonderful Canada is.

The people I've talked to know about Canada on a humanitarian level and they appreciate our role in the world. They see Canada as a generous country of people ready and willing to help others around the world, sending peace keepers into war zones or assisting with disasters. In my younger days, when I traveled with the CBC chasing international stories, the image of Canada as a pure, untouched country fascinated the people I met in other countries. I remember being asked how I could live in such a cold climate. Or whether I knew any Eskimos, as they were then called. They knew Niagara Falls, our enormous lakes and rivers, and the endless forests and snowy landscapes.

But I have never heard spoken the phrase, "Canada has made so many great films." We know how to speak out against injustice, but we haven't yet learned to raise our voices when it comes to telling our stories on the big screen in a way that resonates with audiences around the world.

Our Untold Stories

Why have Canadians made so few films that have broken through internationally? How come we don't have a film where we can expect audiences to say "Oh yeah, that was a great Canadian film." After all, when we hear about *Breaker Morant* or *The Adventures of Priscilla Queen of the Desert, Gallipoli*, we think "Oh yeah, great Australian films." *The Piano, or Once We Were Warriors* are lovely New Zealand films and when I think *City of God* it immediately says Brazil. Canadians have made so many wonderful films, but my point is, who knows about them beyond our borders? Of course we know Italian films; we know German or French films. How about Canadian films?

There have been so many amazing events of international interest from this country that should have been celebrated in our films but we have done nothing with them. In that regard, it's really a shame.

For example, in 1979, our Canadian Embassy in Iran gave six American diplomats shelter and Ken Taylor, the Canadian ambassador in Teheran, gave them refuge in his home. It was a very difficult time for Americans and Canadians harboured the diplomats at a great risk, giving them safe passage out of the country by issuing them false Canadian passports. I got involved with that story because I shot a CBC special documentary, not long after the event. We filmed and interviewed the Americans who had escaped from Iran with the help of the Canadian Embassy. These people were then stationed all over the world with their US embassies – from Sweden, to Hong Kong, still working for the State Department and I thought *Wow, what a great story for the big screen.* I spoke to the freelance producer who had come to CBC with the documentary idea in the first place and I said "Why don't we develop this as a screenplay for a feature film?" Despite a show of interest, nothing happened with that particular producer, or with a few other people I talked to about it either. Eventually, a TV movie was made, but in typical Canadian fashion, it was done on a small scale and very much underplayed. I knew it could be a major film – it was an exciting and important story. Years later, Hollywood got hold of it and the rest is history. The film *Argo* walked away with three Oscars and to me, it was only an okay film with a false perspective on the events. It's a Canadian story – why didn't we make that film?

David Milgaard is another example. I did the two-hour documentary on him in 1992 called *The David Milgaard Story*, shortly after he was released and compensated by the Supreme Court of Canada for spending twenty-three years in prison on a wrongful conviction. That was a strong narrative to be sure, but another story that was equally compelling to me was the story of his mother, Joyce Milgaard. At first Joyce wasn't convinced that David hadn't killed the nurse because she knew of his hippy generation wild-child personality, but when he tried to escape from prison and ended up in hospital with what were thought to be fatal gunshot wounds, she paid him a visit. Joyce listened to David say over and over again, "Mom, I didn't do it, I didn't do it." That's when she realized that her son was telling the truth, even becoming a sleuth herself, uncovering evidence that helped to exonerate her son. She jumped onto his defence, and it is a beautiful story of a mother's unconditional love for her son. I felt this had the potential to be an incredible story of injustice and the fight to prove one's innocence, in the vein of *In the Name of the Father*. Again, we didn't make the film. I talked to many people but I wasn't established at that time and I didn't have the knowledge or clout to develop it myself.

Ben Johnson is another story. When he ran the 100-Metres in the 1988 Seoul Olympics, I was in Australia at the time. I remember being in the pub when he ran and when he won, the crowds cheered, "Good on you, mate," and "Bloody good show, mate," because they wanted Canadians to win, not the Americans. Then the next day or the day after that, I was in New Zealand and there was enormous sadness, "Oh, what a bloody shame," when he was stripped of his Gold Medal. I was able to see how much Canada was loved and how the Aussies and Kiwis wanted Canadians to succeed. So I came back and talked to producers in Toronto about the potential of this amazing bittersweet story, but nothing ever happened. I am sure there are many other stories that can be translated into successful films for the international market.

We know how to tell small, local stories, but when it comes to something that can resonate among wider audiences internationally, we seem to shy away from celebrating Canada and great stories emanating from here.

The same is true of novels and stories written by Canadian authors. Whether it's Michael Ondaatje's *The English Patient*, Yann Martel's *The Life of Pi* or Margaret Atwood's *The Handmaid's Tale*, there is now a long history of American producers telling stories that originated with Canadian authors. Why can't Canadian producers find a way to get these stories out into the world?

That's why a film called "Jack of Diamonds" is at the top of my major to-do list right now. It is about a Canadian geologist in the 1930s, Jack Williamson, who went to Rhodesia in Africa and became the richest man in the world. Legend has it that he would get 3,000 letters a month from women proposing marriage to him. Not only was he rich, but he was handsome too. The most interesting conflict in the story is the way he challenged Ernest Oppenheimer, the South African industrialist who controlled the De Beers diamond monopoly. I think it is a fascinating example of an easy-going Canadian who got pushed around and came out swinging – one might even get the impression that Canadians are pushovers until a certain time when we need to prove ourselves.

Jack was the embodiment of the Canadian character, in

my mind. The question is, why haven't we celebrated Jack Williamson yet? I feel we are our own worst enemies – and I hope I can turn that around before my life is over. Part of the Canadian spirit is our quiet humility, but, at the same time, I feel we need to celebrate ourselves a bit more and share our values with the world.

Staying Small

I have been working in the Canadian film industry for over fifty years and I have enjoyed every minute of my time. I feel lucky and there is nothing I would change about how my career has gone. Yet, at times I've felt some dissatisfaction with how Canada's film industry works. On the one hand, it is wonderful that we have funding organizations that help out Canadian filmmakers and artists. I have worked with most of them at one time or another and I am truly grateful that they have supported my work. At the same time, I wonder if these organizations are giving incentives toward a certain approach to storytelling at the expense of the kind of films that would really put Canada on the map. No one is forced to take money from these sources, but the fact that it is available creates a temptation for filmmakers – and even more so for film producers – to cohere to certain standards that I believe are accidentally hindering Canada's film output as a whole.

When I did my film *Partition*, I was blessed to have the support of Telefilm and other Canadian broadcasters. They liked the project and generously supported it. At the same time, they had their own mandate and insisted that the film – which takes place entirely in India – be shot eighty percent in Canada. It was a difficult task. Due to the talents of our production team, we made it work and the film turned out well. But I question whether it was the right decision for the film. After all, if we had shot the whole thing in India, I could have done it for a much smaller budget, or turned the money we had into a much bigger film. Then again, I fully understand Telefilm's position. They want to keep Canadians employed, so the money comes with conditions. They have every right to make their demands. The problem is, these conditions encourage us to tell a certain type of story. This can be good for 'small films', but all these guidelines make it difficult to make interesting larger-than-life films – the kind of films that would really break through around the globe.

***

Canadians have been very good at exploring issues in our films, but the fact is, when people pay ten or fifteen dollars for a ticket to the movies, they want to escape from worrying about things all the time; they want to be entertained too. That's what Americans are so good at; they market their roller-coaster stories to the whole world.

As Canadian filmmakers, we have every reason to celebrate excellence but still tend to get bogged down with doom and gloom. We can tell great stories, but they always gravitate toward tragedy or some kind of a sad issue. It is important to find a good balance that isn't all fluff like your average American roller-coaster ride entertainment, but that has some substance too. This is in part because of what I mentioned above, but I think it is also a part of our culture to pay attention to sadness and problems, instead of focusing on the uplifting aspect of human spirit, giving people hope and joy.

I often think of the films of my first home, India. It is a country that is crowded, poor and separated by class, but the films are full of joy, romance, bright colours, singing and dancing. Meanwhile, Canada is a rich country with everything to be happy about – yet our films are almost always dark and depressing. Do we as people project the opposite of the world around us? Is the sadness of Canada's films a reflection of how good we have it here? I don't know, but I wish Canadian cinema would represent, more often, the positivity and entertainment side of excitement I see in the people.

There is no question we have talent here and no question that this country is the most beautiful canvas on the planet, but the people at the top who control the financing are still a weak link. Instead of being able to commit to an entertainment project, I believe our decision makers let fear get in the way – fears like not fully representing some ideal of what is 'Canadian', fear of political incorrectness where one group or another may be offended, or even a fear that we are mimicking Hollywood too much. When we spend too much time ticking the boxes, we end up with a lot that is good, but very little that is great.

What is more, when we do make great films in this country, there is a reluctance to stand up behind them. We don't make the films people want to watch, so then they don't want to watch something Canadian. The cycle goes on and on, and the result is, in my mind, so much wasted potential.

There are, of course, other reasons. Hollywood being right down the road is a drain on our talent. Many talented Canadians have had a hugely positive impact on Hollywood – from directors like James Cameron and Norman Jewison, to comedians like Jim Carrey and John Candy – but they have done the majority of their work south of the border. What's more, our closeness to America influences our choices in a great many ways. In this area, I am speaking only about English Canadian films. Quebec's French cinema, which in a sense doesn't compete against Hollywood films, has been stronger because language forces it to exist on its own. It's amazing that French Canadian films, with a limited audience, always seem to do well, while English Canada struggles. In English Canada, so we are inundated with movies from our US neighbours that we are afraid – I believe – to make any film that even resembles Hollywood at all. Because we want to be different and unique, we are afraid to entertain.

New Frontiers

Creating a film takes an enormous amount of time and effort. We deal with competing egos and many conflicting ideas of what the film should be. We have to scrounge and beg for money and then battle the elements and the inevitable misfortunes on the production side. There are many moments of doubt and many sleepless nights. The result? If all goes well, we end up with something audiences will enjoy for a few moments. *All that for ninety minutes*, I often think. But the beautiful thing about a film is that it lasts. The films I've worked on will be here long after I'm gone and forgotten and to know that is a wonderful feeling.

There have been a great number of wonderful films made and it's hard to imagine a world without them. *Dr. Zhivago, Lawrence of Arabia, The English Patient, The Fully Monty, Titanic, Mephisto, The Shawshank Redemption, Hear My Song* – the list goes on. I have some very cherished Canadian films too on my list of films that I hold dear. Donald Shebib's *Goin' Down the Road* is a very well executed film, in a very raw and honest style of filming. *The Decline of the American Empire*, directed by Denys Arcand, is a great subject, done with taste and flair. I recently watched the Irish/Canadian co-production *Maudie*, directed by Aisling Walsh, and I thought it was brilliant, all around. *Hello Destroyer*, directed by Kevan Funk, is also a very focused and well-crafted film, although a bit of a downer. Other Canadian films, that I love include *My American Cousin*, directed by Sandy Wilson; *Bon Cop, Bad Cop*, a Quebec film directed by Eric Canuel; *Dead Ringers*, directed by David Cronenberg, and *Away from Her*, directed by Sarah Polley.

When it comes to my favourite movie of all time, the Italian film *Cinema Paradiso*, directed by Giuseppe Tornatore is the film that has stayed with me the most. It celebrates the magic of film through eyes of a little boy who falls in love with movies for the first time. The passion for cinema this film exudes is something I relate to very much. I feel so fortunate that I was able to celebrate filmmaking in a similar way with my documentary *Keepers of the Magic*. It was purely a labour of love and I enjoyed it immensely, particularly because I got to spend time with iconic cinematographers like Vittorio Storaro (*Apocalypse Now, The Last Emperor, The Conformist*), John Seale (*Witness, Mad Max: Fury Road, The English Patient*) and Gordon Willis (*The Godfather, All the President's Men, Manhattan*) and others. It was wonderful to sit with these great artists and share our love of cinema and it felt good to make a film that was purely about celebrating something we love.

Now I want to shine the same light on Canada. I know my remaining time is limited, so it's very important for me to celebrate this country's landscape, culture, people and its endless stories, from the pioneering days to the present. I want to tell big stories that are worthy of the dramatic landscape Canada has to offer. I love the north, endless prairie fields and railroad tracks, abandoned towns and grain elevators, beautiful prairie sunsets, the beautiful coastline of B.C., the rugged island of Newfoundland – landscape beauty is amazing for me and it is poetry for the camera, a big wonderful canvas on which to paint our pictures. Canada has every reason to create, for itself, the big, exciting films that made me fall in love with movies in the first place. We have all the talent and materials we need. But we have to show the world who we are.

I want us – both myself and other Canadian filmmakers – to tell Canadian stories that will entertain and show the world the Canadian spirit I fell in love with many years ago. If we can be louder in celebrating ourselves as Canadians, the rest of the world will get to see the spirit of this country as I saw it when I first came here.

***

I thought at one point, maybe when I was twenty-one or so, that I wanted to make lots of money in life and be known. It did not take me long to realize that no, there has got to be something else. Fame is an empty feeling that doesn't give one any lasting happiness. And money? How much does one need? I have only one stomach and only need a bed, six feet by four feet on which to rest. I decided at a young age that what I wanted to do is experience life. How lucky I am that I am in a business that allows me to explore life like this. With a camera, I can go up to any door, open it, and say, "I want to tell your story," and they let me come in. I cover poverty, I cover richness, I cover political stories, I cover anything I want – the whole canvas. That's what makes my life rich and I am so grateful for that. How would I have otherwise had a chance to talk to Indira Gandhi or the Dalai Lama? My camera allowed me to do that. Or to meet Pierre Trudeau, or John Lennon? My camera allowed me to do that too.

We, as humans, from the beginning of life, have one thing that drives us. Seeking. We seek happiness, we seek love, we seek good food – always seeking. That's what we do. All of us. Seeking is our main profession, from the time we are born to the time we die. We never stop doing that. And film has allowed me to seek new knowledge, continually opening new doors. Each film takes me to a place I have never been before. When I open a door to a new film I always think, Oh my God, there is so much to learn.

Acknowledgements

Many years ago I interviewed Dawa Tenzing, a Sherpa, and during our interview, at one point I told him that he was a great man. He turned and said to me that I was also great. Needless to say, I felt embarrassed. I tried to change the subject but he came back at it again and said, "I am only as good as you are, and you are only as good as I am, but together we are much stronger." I have never forgotten that thought.

This has been a great journey and I am grateful to so many who have been so good to me: my parents and my brother who have been the emotional foundation of my life and then my children who allowed me to build that house, Dave Brown, Mrs. Campbell, Gail Carr, Ian Challis, Adrienne Clarkson, Suzanne Cook, Bruce Cowley, Jon Dippong, Jeannine Locke, Terrance McEvoy, Neville Otley, Tina Pehme, Kim Roberts, Ray Sager, Diane Sarin, Gordon Stewart, Ken Welsh, Anne Wheeler, Christopher Zimmer, and others who helped me to fill my house with great memories.

It all became a reality, because of this great land we call Canada and the CBC.

Lastly, but most importantly I thank Lorene Shyba as it was her interest and work that made this book possible. I am very grateful for this gift,

Eyepiece Index

Colour Pages are not indexed.

Books in the
'Reflections' Series

A Painful Duty
Forty Years at the Criminal Bar

Book One in the Reflections Series
By C.D. Evans

In *A Painful Duty*, C.D. Evans reveals insights into the practice and the characters of the Criminal Bar, with special tributes to no-nonsense judges.

Price: $42.50 *Trade Paperback*
16 pages of colour photos
ISBN: 978-0-9689754-3-5 (2010)

Less Painful Duties
Reflections on the Revolution in the
Legal Profession

Book Two in the Reflections Series
By C.D. Evans

C.D. Evans reflects on revolutionary changes that have come about within the Canadian legal profession, in particular the Criminal Bar, over the past fifty years; including ascendancy of women in the profession, the Canadian Charter and impacts of technology.

Price: $29.95 *Trade Paperback*
ISBN: 978-0-9952322-1-1 (2017)

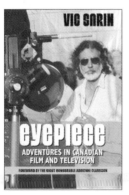

Eyepiece
Adventures in Canadian Film
and Television

Book Three in the Reflections Series
By Vic Sarin
Foreword: The Rt. Hon. Adrienne Clarkson

Vic Sarin highlights many of his over 150 documentary and dramatic films. His trailblazing approach to filmmaking is remarkable and inspiring.

Price: $35.00 *Trade Paperback*
16 pages of colour photos
ISBN: 978-1-988824-02-4 (2017)

 **DURVILE** & Durvile.com
PUBLICATIONS UpRoute
Books and Media

Tough Crimes: True Cases by Top Canadian Criminal Lawyers

Book One in the True Cases Series
Eds: CD Evans and Lorene Shyba

Tough Crimes is a collection of thoughtful and insightful essays from some of Canada's most prominent criminal lawyers. Stories include wrongful convictions, reasonable doubt, homicides, and community.

Price: $29.95 *Trade Paperback*
ISBN: 978-0-9689754-6-6 (2014)

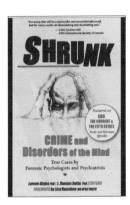

Shrunk: Crime and Disorders of the Mind

Book Two in the True Cases Series
Eds: Drs. Lorene Shyba and J. Thomas Dalby
Foreword: Dr. Lisa Ramshaw

Shrunk is a collection of chapters by eminent Canadian and international forensic psychologists and psychiatrists who write about mental health issues they face and what they are doing about it.

Price: $29.95 *Trade Paperback*
ISBN: 978-0-9947352-0-1 (2016)

More Tough Crimes: True Cases by Canadian Judges and Criminal Lawyers

Book Three in the True Cases Series
Eds: William Trudell and Lorene Shyba
Foreword: Hon. Patrick LeSage

More Tough Crimes provides a unique window into the world of criminal justice. Many cases are recent, but some from the past were so disturbing they resonate in the public consciousness.

Price: $29.95 *Trade Paperback*
ISBN: 978-09947352-5-6 (2017)

Women in Criminal Justice: True Cases by Canadian Judges and Lawyers

Upcoming!

Book Four in the True Cases Series
ISBN: 978-0-9947352-4-9

 &   Durvile.com

5000 Dead Ducks
Lust and Revolution in the Oilsands

A Novel
By C.D. Evans and L.M. Shyba

5000 Dead Ducks is a comedy satire about an unscrupulous group of 'Candidian' lawyers who engineer a revolution to take over the 'Alberia' oilsands.

Price: $16.95 *Trade Paperback*
16 illustrations
ISBN: 978-0-9689754-4-2 (2013)

Stop Making Art and Die
Survival Activities for Artists

By Rich Théroux

The first adult activity book that makes it impossible not to succeed and flourish as an artist. As well as telling a compelling story, Rich Théroux encourages a deeper understanding of art.

Price: $24.95 *Trade Paperback*
ISBN: 978-0-9947352-2-5 (2016)

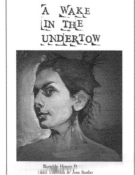

A Wake in the Undertow
Rumble House Poems

By Rich Théroux and Jess Szabo

This gem reveals two people in love as they disclose things survived and dig deep for sacred weapons.

Arms flung wide | Rib cages swung open
Hearts thunder | Wild vibrations
Where that river | meets the ocean.
Welcome home.

Price: $16.95 *Trade Paperback*
Illustrations throughout
ISBN: 978-0-9952322-4-2 (2017)

 &   Durvile.com

RumbleSat Art from the Edge of Space

Edited and Curated by Jim Parker, Lorene Shyba, Rich Théroux

Celebrates the two RumbleSat Art in Space missions; the Canadian Space Agency AUSTRAL 2017 campaign, and the JP Aerospace AWAY 123 launch. Featured in the book is the art of over 100 artists along with stories, and comics by the artists and curators.

Trade Paper, $29.95 | E-book $19.95 | Full colour plates
ISBN: 978-1-988824-04-8 (2017)

Shadow Hymns: Photography by Austin Andrews

Shadow Hymns is an exploration of photojournalism and foreign correspondence by filmmaker Austin Andrews. Photo spreads in the book include Desert Sundials: Angles on the sand seas of Namibia; Pyramiden: Midnight latitudes of Svalbard, and Frontier Empire of Ascension Island. Austin Andrews has profiled stories on six continents for *TIME, Foreign Policy, Maclean's* and *Intersection*, and in the online *National Geographic*.

Trade Paper, $29.95 | E-book $19.95 | Full colour plates
ISBN: 978-1-988824-06-2 (2017)

Upcoming!

LIVING IN THE TALL GRASS
A Poetry Manifesto of Reconciliation | **By Chief R. Stacey LaForme**
ISBN: 978-1-988824-05-5

THE TREE BY THE WOODPILE and other stories
A Dene First Nation Spirit of Nature Tales | **By Raymond Yakeleya**
Illustrations, Deborah Desmarais | *Translation: Jane Modeste*
ISBN: 978-1-98882-40-3

 & Durvile.com